LIFE OF VISCOUNT BOLINGBROKE

London
SIMPKIN, MARSHALL AND CO., LTD.

New York
LONGMANS, GREEN AND CO., FOURTH AVENUE,
AND THIRTIETH STREET.

LIFE OF
VISCOUNT BOLINGBROKE

BY

ARTHUR HASSALL, M.A.

STUDENT OF CHRIST CHURCH, OXFORD

Oxford

B. H. BLACKWELL, BROAD STREET

MCMXV

Henry St. John

PREFATORY NOTE.

No apology is needed for the reissue of a short *Life of Bolingbroke*, which was published in The Statesmen Series in 1889.

Since 1889 much new light has been thrown on the history of the period in which Bolingbroke lived, and consequently it has become necessary to rewrite a considerable portion of the original Life.

Bolingbroke was so closely connected with all the political, literary, philosophical, and social movements of his day, that the history of his career is to a great extent that of the first half of the eighteenth century. It is, therefore, impossible within the small limits of this Prefatory Note to do more than briefly indicate some of the principal sources of information which have been consulted in rewriting this volume:

Dr. Goldsmith's *Life of Henry, Lord Viscount Bolingbroke*, in the 1809 edition of Bolingbroke's Works; G. W. Cooke's *Memoirs of Lord Bolingbroke*, 2 vols.; Rémusat's *L'Angleterre au Dix-huitième Siècle*; T. Macknight's *Life of Lord Bolingbroke*; T. E. Kebbel's *Essays upon History and Politics*; J. Skelton's *Essays in History and Biography*; R. Harrop's *Bolingbroke, a Political Study and Criticism*; J. Churton Collins's *Bolingbroke, an Historical Study*; W. Stebbing's *Verdicts of History Reviewed*; Kussch, *Peterborough*; Wilson, *Life of Berwick*; Morley, *Voltaire*; Craik, *Life of Swift*; Wyon, *History of the Reign of Queen Anne*, 2 vols.; Coxe, *Life of Walpole and Life of Pelham*; Ballantine, *Carteret*; Leslie Stephen, *Pope*; Foss, *Lives of the Judges*; Clarendon, *History of the Great Rebellion*; Gardiner, *History of England*; Marshall's *Genealogical Guide*; C. Grant

v

Robertson, *England under the Hanoverians*; *The Edinburgh Review*, vol. cxxv.; Leadam, *The Political History of England*, 1702 to 1760; *The Dictionary of National Biography*; *The Cambridge Modern History*; *Social England*; W. Sichel, *Bolingbroke and His Times*, 2 vols., 1901; Yorke, *Life of Lord Hardwicke*, 3 vols., 1913.

For those who desire to realize thoroughly the feelings and temper of the age, and Bolingbroke's relations to the world of politics and literature, a perusal of the following will be necessary:

Burnet, *History of My Own Time*; *Letters and Despatches of the Duke of Marlborough, from* 1701-1712. *The Works and Correspondence of Bolingbroke*; *The Private Correspondence of the Duchess of Marlborough*; *Swift's Correspondence*, several of his works, and especially his *Journal to Stella*; *The Memoirs of the Duke of Berwick*; *The Memoirs of De Torcy*; *The Lockhart Papers*; *The Craftsman*; *Pope's Correspondence with Swift and Bolingbroke*; *The Marchmont Papers*; *Letters of Bolingbroke to Madame de Ferriol and to the Abbé Alari* (published in 1808 by Grimoad); *The Stuart Papers*; *The Onslow Papers*; *The Wentworth Papers*; *Somers Tracts*; *Carlisle Papers*; *Portland Papers*; *Harley Papers*.

Even those numbers of *The Craftsman*, which were not written by Bolingbroke or Pulteney, are very well worth perusal, and are calculated to enable us to realize fully the nature of the questions which occupied the public mind, as well as the policy of the Opposition during a great portion of Walpole's Ministry.

From the Very Rev. T. B. Strong, Dean of Christ Church, I received much valuable help in Chapter X. In fact, the latter portion of that chapter is to a very great extent his work. To the courtesy of the Rev. Andrew Clark, Fellow of Lincoln College, and editor of the Oxford Matriculation Registers, I owe some very interesting facts which tend to throw fresh light on the knotty question of Bolingbroke's career at Oxford. To the late Mr. H. O.

Wakeman, Fellow of All Souls' College, I was indebted for much invaluable criticism while writing the Life in 1889. In preparing the present reissue of the volume, I have received considerable assistance from my colleague, Mr. K. G. Feiling, late Fellow of All Souls' College, and now Student of Christ Church.

A. H.

OXFORD,
August, 1915.

TO THE STUDENTS:

The fact that this volume is being used by the Christian Heritage College does not mean that the school necessarily endorses its contents from the standpoint of morals, philosophy, theology, or scientific hypotheses. The position of Christian Heritage College on these subjects is well known.

In order to standardize class work, it is sometimes necessary to use textbooks whose contents the school cannot wholly endorse. You understand, of course, that acceptable textbooks in certain academic fields are very difficult to secure.

CHRISTIAN HERITAGE COLLEGE
San Diego, California

CONTENTS.

CHAPTER I.

HENRY ST. JOHN'S YOUTH AND EARLY PARLIAMENTARY SUCCESSES.

1678-1704.

Henry St. John's birth—Position of Louis XIV., 1678—State of Politics in England—The Manor House at Battersea—St. John's ancestors—Importance of the St. John family during the Great Rebellion—His Father—His early life at Battersea—Eton—Was he at Christ Church?—His grand tour and residence at Paris—His marriage and entry into Parliament—His appearance and eloquence—Party struggles in 1701 and 1702—The Protestant Succession and the balance of power in Europe—St. John takes a prominent position in the House of Commons—Impeachment of the Whig Ministers—The Kentish Petition—Louis XIV.'s recognition of the Pretender—Excitement in England—Death of William III.—Declaration of War—St. John is made an Honorary Doctor at Oxford—Comparison of the views of the Whigs and Tories—The extreme Tories gradually cease to support the war—Godolphin and Marlborough look to the moderate Tories—Occasional Conformity Bill—Ashby *versus* White—Relations between the Lords and the Commons strained—St. John's violent conduct—Parliament prorogued, April, 1704 . . . . . *page* 1

CHAPTER II.

ST. JOHN SECRETARY-AT-WAR AND AFTER.

1704-1710.

The extreme Tories leave the Government—Harley, St. John, and other moderate Tories are given places—Brilliant successes abroad—St. John's close relations with Marlborough—Elections of 1705—Whigs have majority in Parliament—Marlborough and Godolphin adopt Whig view of England's foreign policy—Harley intrigues against the Ministers—St. John's attitude—The Gregg scandal—Resignation of Harley, St. John, Harcourt, and Mansell, 1708—Ministry becomes entirely Whig

ix

CHAPTER III.

BOLINGBROKE'S DIPLOMACY : THE PEACE OF UTRECHT.

1710–1713.

CHAPTER IV.

THE SUCCESSION QUESTION.

1713–1714.

CHAPTER V.

BOLINGBROKE IN EXILE.

1714–1725.

CHAPTER VI.

THE OPPOSITION TO WALPOLE.

1725–1742.

CHAPTER VII.

BOLINGBROKE'S LATER YEARS.

1742-1751.

CHAPTER VIII.

REVIEW OF BOLINGBROKE'S CAREER AND CHARACTER.

CHAPTER IX.

BOLINGBROKE'S LITERARY FRIENDSHIPS.

CHAPTER X.

BOLINGBROKE'S POLITICAL, PHILOSOPHICAL, AND THEOLOGICAL OPINIONS.

CHAPTER XI.

CONCLUSION.

HENRY ST. JOHN,
VISCOUNT BOLINGBROKE

CHAPTER I

HENRY ST. JOHN'S YOUTH AND EARLY PARLIA-
MENTARY SUCCESSES.

1678-1704.

Henry St. John's birth—Position of Louis XIV., 1678—State of Politics
in England—The Manor House at Battersea—St. John's ancestors—
Importance of the St. John Family during the Great Rebellion—His
father—His early life at Battersea—Eton—Was he at Christ Church?—
His grand tour and residence at Paris—His marriage and entry into
Parliament—His appearance and eloquence—Party struggles in 1701
and 1702—The Protestant Succession and the balance of power in
Europe—St. John takes a prominent position in the House of Commons
—Impeachment of the Whig Ministers—The Kentish Petition—
Louis XIV.'s recognition of the Pretender—Excitement in England—
Death of William III.—Declaration of War—St. John is made an
Honorary Doctor at Oxford—Comparison of the views of the Whigs
and Tories—The extreme Tories gradually cease to support the war—
Godolphin and Marlborough look to the moderate Tories—Occa-
sional Conformity Bill—Ashby *versus* White—Relations between the
Lords and the Commons strained—St. John's violent conduct—
Parliament prorogued, April, 1704.

HENRY ST. JOHN was born at Battersea in October, 1678,
and was baptized on the tenth of that month. The year of
his birth augured a stormy future. In August, the Peace
of Nimeguen had been signed, and Louis XIV. had reached
the height of his power. During the next ten years, by his

aggressive and ambitious policy, he endangered the balance of strength in Europe. St. John was destined to assist Marlborough in carrying out the operations employed so successfully to reduce the pretensions of the Bourbons, and to lower the pride of Louis XIV. He was destined in 1712 to be received in France as the pacificator of Europe, as the statesman who would enable an exhausted country to make an honourable peace. That peace itself proved to be both the greatest monument of his fame and one of the principal reasons of his exile.

The events of the autumn of 1678 in England were no less destined to colour his whole future. The discovery of the so-called Popish Plot in August caused the wildest excitement. The impeachment of Danby, and the dissolution of the Long Parliament of the Restoration were followed, in 1679, by that endeavour to exclude the Duke of York from the Crown, which led to the formation of the Whig and Tory parties. The whole history of Bolingbroke's life, from his entry into Parliament in 1701 to his death in 1751, is, without any exaggeration, the history of the Tory party, of its triumph in 1710, of its failure in 1714, of its long years in the cold shade of Opposition, and finally of its reconstruction.

His birth took place in the old Manor House, which was pleasantly situated near the Thames. "The family seat," wrote Hughson in 1808, in his *Circuit of London*, "was a venerable structure, which contained forty rooms on a floor. A large portion of the house was pulled down in 1778. The part left standing forms a dwelling-house: one of the parlours fronting the Thames is lined with cedar, beautifully inlaid, and was the favourite study of Pope, the scene of many a literary conversation between him and his friend Bolingbroke."

In this family mansion resided his grand-parents, Sir Walter St. John and Lady Joanna, with whom lived their son Henry St. John and his wife the Lady Mary, second daughter and joint heiress of the Earl of Warwick. On his mother's side the future Viscount Bolingbroke could claim descent from the great family of D'Eu, distinguished in Normandy before the invasion of England by William the Conqueror. On his father's side he sprang from a race no less ancient or renowned. William St. John is said to have held an important post at the battle of Hastings, and one of his sons added to the wealth no less than to the glory of the name of St. John by his prowess in the wars against the Welsh. He was possessed of the Manor of Stanton St. John in Oxfordshire, and gave the site of the Convent at Godstow. His great-granddaughter and heiress, Mabel, married Adam de Port, the Lord of Basing in Hampshire, a member of an old English family illustrious in pre-Norman times. The son of this marriage, William, took, in the reign of John, his mother's name, and styled himself William de St. John, Lord of Basing, and son and heir of Adam de Port.

During the thirteenth, fourteenth, and fifteenth centuries the family became prominent. In Henry III.'s reign, John St. John, who held the barony of Stanton, was appointed an itinerant justice for Oxfordshire, and his son Roger was killed at the battle of Evesham. Under Henry V. Sir John St. John was Mayor of Bordeaux. In the reign of Henry VI. Oliver St. John married Lady Margaret Beauchamp, sister of Lord Beauchamp, and acquired the lordships of Bletso and of Lydiard Tregoze. On the death of her husband, Lady Margaret married the Duke of Somerset, and their daughter, by her union with Edmund Tudor, Earl of Richmond, became the mother of Henry VII. The east window in Battersea Church, containing portraits of Henry VII., his grandmother Margaret Beauchamp, and Queen Elizabeth, still commemorates the alliance of the St. Johns with the Tudors. After the reign of Elizabeth, the two main

branches into which the family was then divided, became
very prominent in public life. Oliver St. John, Lord of
Bletso, son of the first Lord St. John of Bletso, who was
created a baron in 1559, was as Lord-Lieutenant of Bed-
fordshire warned in 1614 on account of his coolness with
regard to the benevolence which James I. was attempting to
levy in the counties. His son Oliver was created by James
in 1624 the first Earl of Bolingbroke, and, during his lifetime, Charles I. elevated his son to the House of Lords as
St. John of Bletso. In spite of these marks of royal favour,
the Earl showed a " mutinous disposition." In 1626, when
Charles attempted to raise a forced loan, fifteen or sixteen
of the Peers, among whom was Bolingbroke, refused to
lend; and later both father and son espoused heartily the
Parliamentary cause, the Earl being one of the Peers who
were " all of the Presbyterian dye." During the Civil War
the Earl acted as a commissioner of the Admiralty, and,
after figuring as a member of the Assembly of Divines and
as a Joint Commissioner of the Great Seal, died in 1646.

His son was killed at Edgehill, leaving two sons, each of
whom succeeded in turn to the family honours. The elder,
who married a daughter of the Duke of Newcastle, died in
1689, and the younger in 1711. Both seem to have taken
considerable part in the ordinary county business of Bed-
fordshire. The peerage, which became extinct in 1711, was
revived in 1712 in the person of Henry St. John, the subject
of this memoir.

During the seventeenth century the younger line, which
held Lydiard Tregoze, was also winning renown. A turbulent member of the family, Oliver St. John, distinguished
himself in the Irish wars of Elizabeth and of James I., was
appointed a Commissioner for the settlement of Ulster, and
ruled Ireland as Lord Deputy from 1614 to 1622, becoming
in 1621 an Irish Peer with a title of Viscount Grandison.
In 1624 he was one of the Council of War in England, and

in 1626 he was created an English Peer with the title of Baron Tregoze, receiving grants of the manors of Battersea and Wandsworth.

His great-nephew William, second Viscount Grandison, is well known to readers of Clarendon. After fighting gallantly for the king, he died in 1644 at Oxford of wounds received at the siege of Bristol, and left the Battersea estates to his uncle, Sir John St. John. Three of Sir John's sons died for the Crown, and after the death of a grandson the family estates reverted to a younger son of Sir John, Walter, who married Joanna, daughter of Oliver St. John, the Chief Justice of the Common Pleas.

This Oliver, grandson of Thomas, a younger son of the first Lord St. John of Bletso, had as a young lawyer shown as early as 1629 a strong disposition to support the cause of Parliament. He became famous in 1637 as the defender of John Hampden in the case of Ship Money. In the autumn of 1640 he and Pym drew up the Petition of the Twelve Peers for a Parliament, and, in spite of his appointment by Charles to the post of Solicitor-General, remained true to his principles, took a prominent part in attacking Strafford, and supported all the violent measures of the Long Parliament. In 1648 he was appointed Chief Justice of the Common Pleas. He occupied an influential position during Cromwell's Protectorate, and on Cromwell's death was named one of the Council of State.

The marriage of his daughter Joanna to Sir Walter St. John seemed destined to restore harmony in the family. In the Manor House at Battersea the Lady Joanna's grandson, Henry St. John, was brought up. The memory of Sir Walter and Lady Joanna lingered long in Battersea. By the former the church was repaired and a free school founded and endowed. In 1708 Sir Walter died, leaving behind him a character for moderation, kindliness, and public spirit. His wife, the patroness of celebrated preachers like Simon Patrick, of learned theologians like Dr. Manton, and of eccentric Nonconformists like Daniel Burgess, seems to have been of a sterner type than her husband. In her was exemplified the stern puritanical spirit of the Parliamentary lawyer.

Under the care of these worthy people Henry St. John, who was born in October, 1678, passed his early years. Of his mother we know little. When he was but six years old his father, Sir Henry St. John, who led an idle life of pleasure, killed in a brawl Sir William Estcourt, pleaded guilty, and with difficulty secured the king's pardon. He seems to have been indifferent to politics, and took no part in the party quarrels of Anne's reign. In the autumn of 1710, just after the appointment of St. John to the post of Secretary of State, at a most exciting epoch in English history, Swift wrote to Stella that St. John's father " is a man of pleasure, that walks the Mall, and frequents St. James's Coffee House and the chocolate houses, and the young son is principal Secretary of State." In 1716, when his brilliant son was an exile, he was created Baron St. John of Battersea, and died in 1742, after a placid life extending over ninety years. On the death of his first wife he had married Angelica Magdalene, daughter of George Pillesary, described as the Treasurer-General of the French Marines, by whom he had three sons and one daughter. The eldest son George acted as Secretary to the English pleni-potentiaries at the Congress of Utrecht, and had the honour of bringing over to England the final draft of the Treaty. He died shortly afterwards, and his brother John succeeded to his expectations. Frederick, the son of this John, inherited in 1751 the honours which the author of the Treaty of Utrecht had obtained, and became Viscount Bolingbroke ; from him is descended the present Viscount.

A gloomy picture has been drawn by some writers of the early life of Henry St. John. He may have been for a time

under the care of Daniel Burgess, who, though a Noncon-
formist, was far from being a sour fanatic. He himself tells
us that he was at times condemned to read the works of
Dr. Manton. In a letter to Pope he says:

> "It puts me in mind of a Puritanical parson, Dr. Manton, who, if I
> mistake not—for I have never looked at the folio since I was a boy, and
> condemned sometimes to read in it—made a hundred and nineteen sermons
> on the cxix. psalm."

And, writing to Swift in 1721, he threatens to make his
next letter as long as one of Dr. Manton's, "who taught my
youth to yawn, and prepared me to be an High Churchman,
that I might never hear him read, nor read him more."

But beyond this fact all that is known of Sir Walter and
Lady Joanna would lead to the conclusion that the young
Henry's early years were passed under kind and thoughtful
guardianship. Of his schooldays at Eton little information
can be gleaned. Walpole was one of his schoolfellows, and
Horace Walpole, in his *Memoirs of the Reign of George II.*,
states that " they had set out as rivals at school." As Walpole was two years St. John's senior, this statement must, in
the absence of other evidence, be received with caution.
After his schooldays at Eton, St. John, it is usually stated,
proceeded to Christ Church and remained there some years.
A few writers, in unhistorical flights of fancy, have ventured
to describe in some detail his life at college; but of his
residence at Oxford there is no absolute proof. The tradition that he was at Christ Church is, however, strong, and
is repeated by almost all his biographers. In a letter
written from Windsor Castle to the Duke of Shrewsbury
on December the 3rd, 1713, Bolingbroke says: " As to
Dr. Freind, I have known him long, and cannot be without
some partiality for him, since he was of Christ Church." In
the autumn of 1702, on the occasion of the Queen's visit to
Oxford, many of the leading Tories were made honorary
Doctors. Among these was St. John, and he was then

entered on the books of Christ Church. It has been suggested that, in consequence of this honour paid to him, he was accustomed to call himself a Christ Church man but that, as a matter of fact, he never had resided in Oxford. Nevertheless, in the absence of positive evidence, it is still possible that the tradition may be true, and that St. John did study for a time at Oxford. In the sixteenth and seventeenth centuries students frequently worked in Oxford without joining a college. Antony Wood states distinctly that in his own day many who came to Oxford not intending to graduate did not matriculate. Poor scholars would follow this course to avoid expense, and a boy of good family like St. John, who came to Oxford with his own tutor, or who read with a tutor of some College, would not necessarily matriculate or live in College. His name would therefore not appear on the Buttery List. Sir Philip Sidney is always said to have been at Christ Church, but his name is not to be found in any of the books of the University or of Christ Church. Sir Harry Vane studied in Oxford, but did not matriculate ; Davenant the poet is said to have been of Lincoln College, because his tutor was a Fellow of Lincoln. There is, however, no evidence that he matriculated. It may then be true that St. John came to Oxford, studied with a Christ Church tutor, never lived within the walls of Christ Church, and left Oxford without having matriculated. He would be spoken of as being of Christ Church, and might consider himself a Christ Church man.

There is little doubt that during these early years he acquired a considerable knowledge of the Greek and Latin languages, especially of the latter ; aided by an unusually good memory and by remarkable powers of concentration, he managed, in all probability before he was twenty years of age, to make himself thoroughly conversant with most of the best Latin authors. One of the most striking characteristics of St. John is his readiness to turn from politics or pleasure to hard study. In 1708 he buried himself with his books in the country. After the failure of 1715 he left Paris to study philosophy in the heart of France. In 1735, disappointed with the course of his struggle against Walpole, he again withdrew to France, where he wrote some of his masterpieces.

In 1697 he was in London, where for some months he led a riotous life in imitation of his cousin, John Wilmot, Earl of Rochester, who had lately died. His sympathy with literature and literary men was even then evidenced by the intimate relations he formed with Dryden. Prefixed to the translation of Virgil, which appeared in July, 1697, was a poetical composition in the shape of some verses of little merit, bearing the signature " H. St. John." The existence of the well-known legends that St. John received one morning from the hands of Dryden the manuscript of the *Ode to St. Cecilia's Day*, and that on another day he was urged to outstay Jacob Tonson, from whom the poet apprehended some rudeness, seems to attest the truth of Pope's statement that St. John was at this time Dryden's friend and protector.

In the autumn of 1697 he left England for a Continental tour of two years. A portion of the time was spent in Italy, but it is probable that he lived the greater part of 1698 and 1699 in Paris, where Lord Jersey, the English Ambassador and a descendant of Viscount Grandison, introduced him to Parisian life and society. There he met Matthew Prior, then Secretary to the Embassy, who was destined to play an important part under St. John in bringing about the Peace of Utrecht. The thorough mastery of the French tongue which St. John acquired during his stay in Paris proved a most invaluable accomplishment during the years he was Secretary of State.

At the beginning of 1700 he returned to England, where he wrote an ode entitled *Almahide*, which, like his earlier efforts, shows that poetry was not his province. His wild and reckless life alarmed his relatives, who seemed conscious that the turbulent and unrestrained vigour of their young kinsman might be utilized. It was hoped that marriage and a seat in Parliament would steady him and turn his attention to politics, then passing through an intensely interesting and exciting phase, worthy of the intellect, energy, and ambition of St. John. At the end of 1700 he married Frances Winchescombe, daughter and one of the coheiresses of Sir Henry Winchescombe, a well-to-do baronet living in Berkshire, and a descendant of Jack of Newbury, so famous in the reign of Henry VIII.

The lady brought St. John considerable wealth, and on the death of her father succeeded to an estate near Reading. Swift, who was much attached to her, tells us how devoted she was to her husband in 1711, though there is no doubt that the harmony of their married life was at times broken by quarrels, which, about the year 1713, appear to have become serious. Still she seems to have loved him faithfully, and after his fall she wrote to Swift that she became furious, if they mentioned her "dear lord without respect." When St. John fled from England in 1715 she did not follow him, and died in 1718, leaving him nothing.

In the Parliament which met on February the 6th, 1701, St. John sat for Wootton Bassett, a family borough in Wiltshire. He at once attached himself to the Tory party, and more particularly to Harley, who was leader of the Tories and Speaker of the House of Commons. Rarely has a Parliament met at a more exciting political crisis; rarely has political opinion swayed backwards and forwards more violently, than during the four years succeeding the Peace of Ryswick. Into the vortex of the struggling parties St. John now plunged, and at once became prominent, acting as a rule with the extreme section of High Churchmen led by Bromley. Nature had supplied him with many advantages. Tall and graceful in his person, his features were elevated, handsome, and refined. His eyes were eager and piercing, his nose aquiline, his forehead lofty, his hair dark brown, his smile sweet and winning. With his commanding presence and his very considerable oratorical powers, St. John was calculated to impress the assembly of which he was now a member. He soon established a reputation as a skilful Parliamentary debater among the Tory mediocrities who surrounded him. With his felicity of expression and his mastery of sarcasm, he combined a tremendous capacity for invective. To his oratory alone he owed his early advancement. Such a power had not been seen on the side of the Tory squires in the House of Commons for many a long day, and as he assailed Somers, Wharton, and Halifax with all his passionate and often ironical eloquence, it is no wonder that he at once secured the admiration and support of the "Young England" Tories. Seldom has a young statesman of St. John's ability found, on entering Parliament, such excellent opportunities for at once taking a leading position.

The whole history of England from February, 1701, to the death of William III. in March, 1702, illustrates what he says in one place, "That we run into extremes always." In 1697 the nation was as anxious to get out of the war as it had been in 1689 to get into it, and, although the great question of the Spanish Succession still awaited solution, it seemed as though England had decided to interfere no more in Continental affairs. Hence many soldiers and sailors were disbanded, the Dutch guards were dismissed, the Partition Treaties were censured, and Philip was recognized by William as King of Spain. Even Louis' acceptance of the will of Charles II., his seizure of the Barrier Towns, and his threatening attitude towards English commerce provoked little alarm. Had he satisfied England in matters of trade and had he kept the terms of the Peace of Ryswick,

Philip would have quietly secured the Spanish empire without opposition from England. But Louis' recognition of the Pretender, in a moment of ill-advised chivalry, provoked the most violent excitement in England, and led directly to the War of the Spanish Succession. St. John himself confessed at a later time that " his notions of the situation of Europe on that extraordinary crisis " were extremely imperfect, and that he saw the true interests of his country in a half-light. And he allowed that he could not see what "King William could do in such circumstances as he found himself in after thirty years' struggle except what he did."

In St. John's first Parliament the two most important questions were the Protestant Succession, and the maintenance of the balance of power in Europe. On these two questions the policy of the Whig party, in whose ranks the young Walpole found himself, was absolutely clear. To prevent at all hazards the return of the Stuarts, to form and uphold a league of European nations which should guarantee the Parliamentary settlement and curb the power of France —was a policy which had the advantage of being intelligible. On the question of settling the Crown in the succession of the House of Hanover the nation was firm, and the Tories, in spite of the evident reluctance of many of their number, were compelled to frame that great constitutional measure —the Act of Settlement. In his account of *The State of Parties at the Accession of King George I.* St. John says with reference to this measure : " The Tories voted for it then ; yet were they not thought, nor did they affect as the others did, to be thought extremely fond of it." And he allows in the same place, that at that time the Whigs acted like the national party. It was in connection with this measure that St. John first came prominently into notice. In spite of his youth he was appointed with the Secretary of State, Sir Charles Hedges, to prepare and bring in the Bill for *The Further Security of the Protestant Succession.*

On the question of the balance of power, the nation was at that moment indifferent, and St. John, after supporting with all his eloquence the views of Harley on the Succession question, attacked with great vehemence the Whig Peers who were held by the Tories to be responsible for the Partition Treaties. Somers, Portland, Halifax, and Orford were, in April, 1701, successively impeached, and only escaped from the violence of the " Young England " Tories by the firm attitude of the House of Lords. St. John's intemperate attitude at that time was brought up against him at a later period when he was complaining of the intolerance of the Whig majority. When the Kentish Petition was presented, he defended the privileges of the House of Commons, which he considered were attacked. St. John himself in later times excused his attitude towards the Partition Treaties on the score of youth and inexperience. The same excuse must serve to explain his fierce attacks on the Petitioners. The factious and intemperate conduct of the Commons in these matters led William to prorogue Parliament in June, and to dissolve it in November. Before the new Parliament met, party struggles had been forced to yield to grave European questions. The violent enthusiasm which, in consequence of Louis' recognition of the Pretender, was in the autumn of 1701 awakened for the Protestant succession, and for a European coalition against France, carried all before it, and the nation declared unmistakably for war. St. John was again returned for Wootton Bassett in the new Parliament which was summoned for December the 30th, 1701. Harley was again elected Speaker, his nomination being seconded by St. John.

In this Parliament, though the Whigs had carried most of the counties and the large towns, parties were pretty evenly balanced. William's stirring speech produced a considerable effect, the Treaties which constituted the Grand Alliance were accepted, and supplies were voted. The

Tory party yielded still further to the popular excitement, and passed measures directly aimed at the House of Stuart and its partisans. The Pretender was attainted of High Treason, and an Abjuration Bill was carried, which compelled all office-holders to acknowledge William III. as the rightful and lawful King, and stigmatized as high treason any attempt to hinder the next heir according to the Act of Settlement from succeeding to the Crown. A considerable portion of the Tory party were opposed to this Bill, and it was only carried by a majority of a single vote. St. John sided, during the debate on this measure, with the party hostile to the Bill. On March the 8th, William III. breathed his last. On May the 15th, war was declared in London, at Vienna, and at the Hague, and Marlborough was made Captain General of the Queen's forces by land and sea. Parliament was dissolved in July, and St. John was a third time elected for Wootton Bassett.

During the recess, Queen Anne, on her way from Windsor to Bath, stopped at Oxford, and that loyal University marked the occasion by conferring Academical honours on leading members of the Tory party. St. John, together with Bromley and Sir Simon Harcourt, were made honorary Doctors, and, in addition, St. John was entered on the books of Christ Church. These marks of distinction seem to show that already St. John had won a reputation remarkable in so youthful a politician.

In October Anne's first Parliament met. For the third time Harley was elected Speaker, and the Tories were in overwhelming strength. They came up to Parliament "in full fury," says Burnet, "against the memory of the late king, and against those who had been employed by him." Most of the ministerial changes made since William's death had been in favour of the Tories. Halifax and Somers were no longer Privy Councillors; Hedges and Nottingham, both Tories, were made Secretaries of State; the Lord

High Treasurership was placed in the hands of the Tory Godolphin, while such pronounced Tories as Dartmouth and Harcourt were chosen Privy Councillors. Thus was laid the foundation of the famous Godolphin Administration, which, after adding a brilliant page to English history, came to a sudden end in 1710. In spite of the moderation of Godolphin and Marlborough, it became at once evident that Parliamentary history had entered upon a stormy period. Till the reconstruction of the Ministry in 1704, the influence of the extreme Tories was in the ascendant, and for two years the relations between the two Houses were more strained than at any previous or subsequent epoch. In the House of Lords the majority, though not large, was decidedly Whig, and under able leaders often proved a serious obstacle to St. John and his supporters. The Whigs were firmly attached to the principles of the Revolution and to the Protestant succession. They were vehemently opposed to France, and regarded the annihilation of Louis XIV.'s power as essential for the independence of England. By an extended system of foreign alliances they hoped to protect the Parliamentary Settlement. The bond which united the Whigs was *political* rather than religious.

In the House of Commons probably three-fourths of the members were Tories. The great aim of the Tories was to undo the effects of the Revolution, and to restablish the predominance of the Church and the landed interest in the government. A hatred of standing armies, a contempt for the new "moneyed" class, the conviction that England should wage war upon the sea alone, indiscriminating attachment to the Church and an undying hatred of Nonconformists—such were the recognized Tory principles. Various views were held as to the royal succession. Probably only a small number were at any time sincere Jacobites. The bond which united the mass of Tories was always *religious* rather than political, and the cry of " the Church in Danger " invariably united the party. While the Tories reflected the views of the Church and the landed interest, the Whigs reflected the sentiments of the middle class, of the merchants, and of the Nonconformists. The Tory party was not, however, united. Already it tended to fall into two divisions of extreme and moderate Tories. Rochester, Jersey, Normanby, and Nottingham in the Lords, Hedges and Seymour in the Commons represented the former section; Harley, Harcourt, and, later, St. John, were the most prominent of the moderate Tories. The peculiar position in which the Tory party found itself on Anne's accession could hardly fail to be the cause of serious disagreement between the two Tory sections. The war was essentially a Whig war: yet the Tories had entered upon it, and, like Walpole in 1739, were carrying on a war opposed to their convictions. They could not deny that the war in its inception was necessary, but they viewed with dislike the obvious results of war,—the augmented taxes, the standing army, the increased influence of contractors, jobbers, and fundholders. Rochester had opposed even the declaration of war on the ground that neither England's commerce nor her security were threatened, and had suggested that the share of England in the war should be confined to the sending of troops to the aid of the Dutch, and perhaps to some pecuniary aid to the Allies. It was evident that Godolphin and Marlborough could not hope to carry on the war successfully while such views were held by members of the Government. They soon saw that their true policy was to look to the moderate Tories for support. But these rocks ahead were hardly foreseen in 1702. At that time the Tories were apparently a united body, engaged in a great struggle with the Whigs over the Occasional Conformity Bill, the introduction of which was entrusted to St. John and two other Tory members.

This measure was framed in absolute accordance with the opinions of the bulk of the Tory party. The Revolution of

1688 had saved the Church from the dangers which threatened her on the side of Rome. The Tories now regarded her in equal danger from the Nonconformists, whose growing prosperity filled them with alarm. To prevent the introduction of Nonconformists into offices of emolument and dignity, and to check their influence on education, was the object of the Bill against Occasional Conformity.

In his *Letter to Sir William Wyndham*, St. John, while allowing that the Bill was "necessary for our party interest," adds that it was

"Deemed neither unreasonable nor unjust. The good of society may require that no person shall be deprived of the protection of the Government on account of his opinions in religious matters; but it does not follow from hence that men ought to be trusted in any degree with the preservation of the Establishment who must, to be consistent with their principles, endeavour the subversion of what is established."

The Bill, supported by the eloquence of St. John, was carried in the Lower, but thrown out in the Upper House. In a subsequent conference held in January, 1703, in the Painted Chamber, between the Lords and the Commons, St. John, as one of the managers for the Lower House, defended the cause of intolerance. Having failed to convince the Lords of the evils attendant on occasional Conformity, the Tories proceeded to attack Halifax, patron of Addison and founder of the Bank of England, who was obnoxious to the Tories as a supporter of the "moneyed" interest. Seven commissioners were appointed to examine the public accounts, and among these seven was St. John. The report of the Commissioners was followed by a direct attack on Halifax; he was voted guilty of gross mismanagement, and only saved from prosecution at the hands of the Attorney-General by the Lords, who absolved him. The Tories in the Lower House, furious at the conduct of the Lords, moved a strong representation to the Queen, and brought forward the question of the resumption of King

William's grants of land, over which there had already been much fierce controversy. They then introduced a Bill, disqualifying placemen from sitting in Parliament. In the debates over these measures St. John found in Robert Walpole, who had already gained the ear of the House, a powerful antagonist. So violent became the dissensions between the two Houses that Anne brought the Session to a close on the 27th of February. In the autumn of 1703 St. John strongly supported the second introduction of the Occasional Conformity Bill, which again was thrown out by the Lords, and about the same period he took a prominent part in attacking the right of the Lords to examine accused persons.

The condition of Scotland was very unsettled, and a plot had been discovered which was thought to aim at the restoration of the Stuarts. The Peers determined to examine the accused persons themselves, and in so doing were opposed by the Tory minority in the Lords, supported by the strong anti-Whig feeling in the Commons. It was determined to search the Lords' Journals on the subject, and St. John, who was one of the members appointed for this purpose, read to the House on the 20th of December the results of the investigations. The Lords defended their position with spirit. In the paper war which followed between the two Houses, St. John played a considerable part, though it would seem that the arguments of Somers, who drew up the addresses of the Lords, were far superior to those of the Commons. In the great struggle over the case of Ashby *versus* White, St. John came prominently forward in opposing the action of the Lords who supported the legal rights of the electors. In his first reported speech, made on the 26th of January, 1704, he declared that he could not think that the liberties of the people would be safer in any hands than those of the House of Commons, or that the influence of the Crown would be stronger there than in the

Courts below. Walpole took the opposite view in defence of the electors, and made a powerful speech against the doctrines brought forward by St. John. So fierce became the contest between Lords and Commons, the former being in harmony with public opinion, that Anne, who had vainly in her Speech at the opening of the Session in November recommended moderation, prorogued Parliament early in April, 1704. So far St. John had identified himself with the most violent section of the Tories, and had, mainly by his oratorical powers, secured a position rarely attained by a politician of the age of five-and-twenty. His genius and ambition had already gained for him distinction in the House of Commons. It remained to be seen if he possessed those business qualities which go far to make a successful Minister.

CHAPTER II

ST. JOHN SECRETARY-AT-WAR AND AFTER.

1704-1710.

The extreme Tories leave the Government—Harley, St. John, and other moderate Tories are given places—Brilliant successes abroad—St. John's close relations with Marlborough—Elections of 1705 ; Whigs have majority in Parliament—Marlborough and Godolphin adopt Whig view of England's foreign policy—Harley intrigues against the Ministers —St. John's attitude—The Gregg scandal—Resignation of Harley, St. John, Harcourt, and Mansell, 1708—Ministry becomes entirely Whig—Failure of Jacobite rising in Scotland—St. John's reasons for his retirement—His life at Bucklersbury—Negotiations at the Hague, 1709—The Battle of Malplaquet—The Barrier Treaty—The Negotiations at Gertruydenberg, 1710—The Sacheverell incident—Reasons of weakness of Whig Ministry : its fall, 1710—Tory Ministry : St. John Secretary of State.

THE year 1704 was to see a great change in the fortunes of St. John. The war was popular and righteous, and received the support, not only of the Whigs, but also of the moderate Tories, in whose ranks Marlborough and Godolphin could still be numbered. But the extreme or High Tories disliked it from the first. Though they had agreed to support the war, they desired to settle, in accordance with their own views, England's relations to the Allies and the manner in which the war should be carried on. They considered England's insular position rendered her incapable of posing on the Continent as a military power. Her strength lay on the sea. Her navy should therefore be made efficient ; her maritime supremacy should be firmly established, and the French ports, commerce, and colonies should be vigorously attacked. Under certain circumstances our Allies might be subsidized, and, should the necessity arise of sending an

armed force to help them in Europe, the scene of our operations should be in Spain, where a victory would rally the
population to our side. One is irresistibly reminded of the
general features of England's foreign policy followed by
Pitt and his successors between 1793 and 1815.

Hatred of standing armies, opposition to a policy of active
intervention on the Continent, dislike of a close alliance
with the Germans and Dutch, remained throughout the war
the sentiments of the extreme Tories. It was impossible,
as the war grew fiercer, and military operations more extended, for them to work, like the Whigs, cordially with
Marlborough and Godolphin, who were convinced that
Louis would overrun Germany, conquer Holland, and
restore the Pretender, if England stood aside and did not
vigorously assist her Allies, especially in the Netherlands.
It is thus easy to understand how it came about that the
history of the reign to 1708 is the history of the gradual
drifting of power to the side of the Whigs, whose views on
foreign policy and on the proper conduct of the war coin-
cided with those of Godolphin and Marlborough. Their
Tory associations, and the Queen's well-known views, however, prevented these Ministers from throwing in their lot
with the Whigs as soon as a breach with the extreme Tories
became inevitable. They preferred to attempt to carry on the
Government by the aid of the more moderate members of the
Tory party. The first sign of the approaching split in the Tory
party appeared in February, 1703, when Ormonde was appointed to succeed Rochester as Lord-Lieutenant of Ireland.

Early in 1704 Jersey and Seymour, both violent Tories,
were deprived of their offices. Nottingham, who had taken
up a position of rivalry to Godolphin, urged in vain the
dismissal of the Dukes of Devonshire and Somerset from
the Privy Council. Finding his influence gone, he resigned
in May, and his resignation was accepted. Blaithwayte, the
Secretary-at-War, followed. Their places were filled for

the most part by moderate Tories; Jersey and Seymour were succeeded by Kent and Mansell, the former a moderate Whig; Harley, who had suggested most of the changes in the Government, succeeded Nottingham as Secretary of State for the Southern Department of Foreign Affairs, and to St. John was given the control of the War Office with the title of Secretary-at-War and of the Marines.

Until 1706 the Government was not strongly partisan. It was based on the principle that the Sovereign had the right to choose the Ministers. Queen Anne, Marlborough, and Harley all desired that, though the Tory element should be supreme, members of both parties should be included in each administration, and, although circumstances combined to force Marlborough and Godolphin in 1708, St. John during the last years of Anne's reign, and the ministers of George I. and George II. to discard this doctrine, it by no means completely died out of English political life. In the middle of the eighteenth century, the degeneration of party into faction led the elder Pitt to attempt to form a Ministry of the ablest men of all parties, while the circumstances of his day and the security of his title enabled George III. at many important crises both to choose and to dismiss his Ministers at his own caprice.

In the reconstitution of the Government in 1704 Harley took a leading part. By birth he was connected with the Nonconformists, and had supported the Revolution. After the Peace of Ryswick he became the leader of the Tories, more by accident than by conviction. Ambitious, and not over-scrupulous, he had no sympathy with their High Church or monarchical views. While, like Burke, anxious to see all royal influence upon the House of Commons abolished, his great aim was to secure the independence of the House of ministerial control. Hence he was strongly opposed to party government with its Cabinet system, and desired to restore the old authority of the Privy Council.

Consequently he was always involved in plots and intrigues against the existing Government, even though he might be a member of the Ministry itself.

He was, moreover, trusted by moderate men of all parties. He had a great reputation for wisdom. He had considerable knowledge of individuals. He was a most successful party manager. His views were not extreme. To Marlborough such a man as Harley was invaluable.

The appointment of St. John, then only twenty-six years old, was more startling. A great European war was raging, and no one could say what the result would be. Blenheim had not yet been won; Marlborough was hampered at every turn by the Allies. At home the Government was face to face with a powerful and angry Opposition. The appointment of so young a man as St. John was a dangerous experiment, especially as he had till lately been regarded as a violent Tory. His biographers ask if his appointment was due to his own abilities, to the influence of Harley, or to the favour of Marlborough. His abilities had been amply proved; he had been a close friend and ally of Harley since he first entered Parliament. But it was mainly to the favour of Marlborough that his appointment was due. There seems little doubt that St. John was well known to, if not a particular favourite of Marlborough. In Letter VII. on *The Study and Love of History* St. John speaks of Marlborough as "that great man, whose faults I knew, whose virtues I admired, and whose memory, as the greatest general and as the greatest Minister that our country or perhaps any other has produced, I honour." Marlborough himself wrote to Godolphin in July, 1704, in the following terms: "I am glad that you are pleased with St. John's diligence; I am confident that he will never deceive you." In later days St. John himself declared that he was indebted neither to Harley nor Marlborough for his appointment, but to the position he had already gained in Parliament. But, whether appointed by interest or merit, he well justified the confidence reposed in him. Though he had hitherto placed his rare oratorical powers at the service of the extreme members of his party, his ambition prevailed over his early political connections, and for four years he acted loyally with the moderate Tories.

From 1704 to 1708, during a period of extraordinary anxiety abroad and of constant and ever-increasing party struggles at home, St. John proved himself possessed of an amount of ability, energy, and calm foresight which marked him out as a leader of men. His first two years of office were rendered famous by reason of a series of marvellous successes abroad. Blenheim, won in August, 1704, saved the Empire and Vienna from French invasion, and placed Bavaria in subjection to the Emperor. Ramillies, fought in May, 1706, secured a barrier for the Dutch against French aggression. The battle of Turin, won by Eugene in September of the same year, saved Savoy, and enabled the Imperial troops to occupy North Italy and Naples. Portugal had joined the Allies as early as 1703 ; Gibraltar had been captured in 1704. In the autumn of 1705 the Archduke Charles had been proclaimed, and accepted as king by a large portion of the Spanish nation. It seemed in 1706 that the neck of the Spanish difficulty was broken. In addition to these disasters to the French cause, the wretched condition of the French finances, Louis' unfortunate choice of generals, and the still smouldering discontent in the Cevennes, all told in favour of the Allies. During these years St. John was in constant correspondence with Marlborough, writing an enthusiastic letter after Blenheim, sympathizing with him over the tiresome conduct of our German and Dutch Allies in 1705, when their dilatoriness prevented the achievement of any marked success in the Netherlands, and congratulating him later on the famous victory of Ramillies. "France and faction," he wrote, "are the only enemies England has to fear, and your grace will conquer both; at least, while you beat the French, you give a strength to the Government which the other dares not contend with."

The brilliant successes abroad seem rather to have intensified than assuaged party conflict at home. It is interesting to mark how the responsibilities of office had changed St. John. From a reckless Tory advocate he had become a moderate, statesmanlike man of business.

In the autumn of 1704 the Tories, never enthusiastic about the war, insisted on coupling with the address of congratulation to Marlborough for the victory of Blenheim congratulations to Rooke, the Tory Admiral, on a drawn battle in the Mediterranean. The more reckless of the Tories then resolved to force the Bill against Occasional Conformity through the House of Lords by tacking it to the Land Tax Bill. In the majority which defeated a motion to that effect St. John's name was found. In the spring of 1705 Parliament was dissolved. The Tories had lost the popularity they enjoyed at the beginning of the reign. Their arbitrary policy towards the Aylesbury voters, which threatened, a few weeks before the dissolution of Parliament, to result in another deadlock between the two Houses, their factious conduct, their jealousy of Marlborough, and their well-known dislike of the war, all tended to throw public feeling on the side of the Whigs. The question before the country was that of foreign policy. And the nation had to decide between an insular and a cosmopolitan policy. The Tory cry, that the Church was in Danger, was of no avail, and in the new Parliament which met in October the Whigs had a majority in both Houses, and a Whig Speaker, Smith, was elected in place of Harley. Anne had already been prevailed upon by Godolphin and the Marlboroughs to dismiss Wright, the Lord Keeper, an old High Church Tory lawyer, and to appoint in his place William Cowper, the most graceful Whig orator in the House of Commons.

St. John had been again returned for Wootton Bassett, and till his resignation in 1708 saw the Tory party commit blunder after blunder, and the Ministry forced to rely more and more on the Whigs for support.

Anne was alienated from the Tories by the proposal of the Tory Peers that the presumptive heir should be invited to reside in England,—a mistake of which the Whigs cleverly took advantage. When Parliament met in December, 1706, the Whigs were stronger than ever. With Godolphin and Marlborough they had come to a fairly definite understanding. In 1707, in spite of the opposition of Rochester, Nottingham, and other extreme Tories, they carried, with the concurrence of the greater part of the moderate Tories, the Union with Scotland, thus defending the Parliamentary Settlement from a danger at home which had begun to be serious. Every fresh success abroad, too, strengthened the Whig party. The war was their war. Each new victory was their victory. And after Ramillies it became evident that it was impossible for the war still to be carried on by Tories. A few weeks after that battle Louis had opened negotiations for peace. By the terms of the Grand Alliance it had been stipulated *that the kingdoms of France and Spain should never be united or governed by the same person, that the Dominions and commerce of the Dutch should be secured, and that a reasonable satisfaction should be given to the Emperor and the English King.* But Louis' proposals were similar to the terms of the Second Partition Treaty, which had been so unpopular in England. He offered a compromise, according to which Philip was to have Naples, Sicily, and Milan. This compromise, which was in many ways unsatisfactory, was rejected by Marlborough and the Emperor.

In Letter VIII. on *The Study of History*, St. John writes

as follows : " It will not, because it cannot, be denied that all the ends of the Grand Alliance might have been obtained by a peace in 1706." He then proceeds to show that France, defeated abroad, was exhausted by the burdens of the war, that the charge of the war to England and Holland was increasing annually, and that a peace in 1706 would have been glorious and satisfactory. This was the view taken by the Tories, and henceforward they strenuously opposed the continuance of the war. The views of the Whigs were clearly shown in a celebrated Resolution which passed both Houses of Parliament in December, 1707, that no peace *" can be safe or honourable for her Majesty and her allies if Spain and the Spanish West Indies be suffered to continue in the power of the House of Bourbon."* The objects of the war were no longer those expressed in the terms of the Grand Alliance. The Whigs had adopted a distinctly new policy, which aimed at the continuance of the war till France was reduced to the position of a second-rate power.

But there was great justification for the Whig view of the danger of permitting the monarchies of France and Spain to be controlled by Bourbons. The fear inspired by Louis XIV. was general, and it was held by Whigs and Tories alike that the King of France must be forced to give up Spain. It was honestly believed, by men as cool and sagacious as Marlborough, that the safety and liberties of Europe would be in immediate danger if Spain and the West Indies were left to the House of Bourbon. The course of events proved conclusively, not only that the Whig fears were chimerical, but that it was impossible to wrest Spain from Philip. The new policy on which England entered in the autumn of 1707 was none the less in harmony with the prevailing ideas of by far the larger portion of the nation.

In his later writings St. John complains bitterly of the Whig change of plan.

"The war was wise and just before the change, because necessary to maintain that equality among the Powers of Europe on which the public peace and common prosperity depends." And, he continues, the war was "unwise and unjust after the change."

At the time, however, St. John made no opposition to the Resolution. As Secretary-at-War he was occupied with the affairs of the English in Spain. In April, 1707, the Allies had suffered an overwhelming defeat at Almanza. It was clear that the Dutch thought only of acquiring towns in the Netherlands, and that the Emperor was indifferent to Spanish affairs so long as he secured his Italian conquests.

If the war was to be continued in Spain, England would have to bear the whole expense. It is obvious that, through the clear-cut division between Whigs and Tories on the question of the continuance of the war, the retention of office by St. John was becoming difficult. The Ministry was now almost entirely Whig, the objects of the war had changed, and the Tories, convinced that the victories of Marlborough, Eugene, and Peterborough had satisfied the ends of the war, opposed its continuance. St. John could not possibly have remained much longer a Tory member of a Whig Ministry. Events, perhaps fortunately, came to his aid and forced him to retire from office.

For some time past Godolphin had been compelled, owing to his compact with the Whigs, to solicit from Anne places of emolument that fell vacant for members of that party. Anne resented this interference, and allowed herself to be influenced by Harley and Abigail Hill in making appointments. In supporting the Queen in her resentment against her leading advisers, Harley was only following his usual course of policy. The elections of 1705 had increased the hopes of the Whigs, and it became obvious that they now aimed at securing an undivided supremacy in the Government. Besides, the clauses in the Act of Settlement which he had introduced, in order to revive the power of the Privy Council as a check on the Cabinet system and on the

Executive Power, had been repealed. He saw too that Marlborough must perforce look more and more to the Whigs for support in his war policy. Nothing remained, then, but to bring about a rearrangement of the administration, in which a more perfect balance of antagonistic interests should be maintained

Harley's intrigues were perfectly justifiable. The Government of 1704 was a Coalition Government, and was recognized as such by both Harley and Marlborough. But from 1706 Marlborough and Godolphin aided the Whigs in their efforts to form a Government almost entirely Whig.

Thus, during a great struggle abroad, when union was of the utmost consequence, the Ministry found itself weakened by the existence of intrigues within its own ranks. As early as the autumn of 1706, keen observers like the Duchess of Marlborough not only knew of the intrigues of Harley and Mrs. Masham, but began to suspect that St. John was also implicated. In October, Godolphin wrote to Marlborough that the Duchess had told him "that Mr. Harley, Mr. St. John, and one or two more of your particular friends were underhand endeavouring to bring all the difficulties they could think of upon the public business in the next session." But Godolphin and Marlborough, by acting in contravention of that arrangement, by which the moderate Tories had taken office in 1704, had no reason to be surprised if attempts were made to turn the tables on them. Their position between the High Tories and the advancing Whigs was certainly a difficult one, but Harley's conduct was as defensible as Marlborough's and Godolphin's.

St. John himself alludes to the intrigues in a letter to Marlborough in November, 1706 :—

"There are," he wrote, "some restless spirits, who are foolishly imagined to be the heads of a party, who make much noise and have no real strength, that expect the Queen, crowned with success abroad, and governing without blemish at home, should court them at the expense of her own authority."

It is very doubtful if St. John was at this time Harley's accomplice. He ends the letter above quoted by assuring the Duke that he has no interest in view but " the Queen's service, and my gratitude and duty to you, who have tied me, for ever." There is no ground beyond the suspicions of the jealous Duchess for thinking that St. John was acting basely. Marlborough was at the height of his power, and, from the lowest point of view, a consideration of his own interests would probably have kept St. John true to his benefactor and friend. The intrigues, however, became serious as time went on. The introduction into the Ministry of Sunderland, Marlborough's son-in-law, as Secretary of State in place of Hedges, tended to alienate the Queen still more from the Duchess. " The only Tories of eminence," writes Mr. Leadam, "left in office were Harley and St. John." All through 1707 it was obvious that Harley was the centre of the intrigues which were opposed to the interests of Marlborough and Godolphin. Sunderland, writing to Marlborough, spoke of him as " the author of all the tricks played here " ; but Harley's own protestations completely deceived the Duke, and he continued to form schemes against the supremacy of Godolphin and Marlborough in the Cabinet. When the first United Parliament of Great Britain met in October, 1707, the Whigs, whose difficulties had been greatly increased by the short-sighted and selfish policy of the Emperor and the Dutch, had serious grounds for complaint as well as for uneasiness. Anne had shown her real leanings by appointing Tories to the sees of Chester and Exeter, and a great loss had just been sustained by the partial destruction of a convoy to Lisbon by a French fleet.

During this session, in which the plan of the war was altered, St. John's labours were very great. The affairs of Spain were under consideration, and he was closely examined as to the condition of the English troops in the Peninsula. He had to show a minute acquaintance with figures and accounts. His frequent statements in Parliament gave ample proof of great administrative powers and of very considerable business qualities. All evidence seems to show that his work had been satisfactorily done. Indeed, throughout his life, distaste to hard work was never one of his failings. Whatever he took in hand was always thoroughly accomplished. His great powers of concentration, his wonderful memory, his power of writing clear business-like letters, all combined to make him an excellent Secretary-at-War. But his labours were drawing to an end. Towards the close of the year Harley's intrigues seem to have developed into a real Bedchamber Plot, the object of which was, according to report, to replace Godolphin by a more pronounced Tory. Swift alludes to this project as " the greatest piece of court skill that has been acted these many years." The Whigs were in a great state of alarm, while in the city the rumour of the removal of Godolphin caused a semi-panic. In this struggle, Harley, Mrs. Masham, and the Queen were pitted against the tyranny of the Marlboroughs backed by the Whig leaders.

On January 29th, 1708, St. John astonished Godolphin and his colleagues by laying before the House of Commons the muster rolls, which showed that at the Battle of Almanza only 8,600 English troops instead of 29,595 were in Spain. In spite of explanations the Ministry had suffered a serious blow.

The Queen's influence on politics was so great that for a time Godolphin and Marlborough, though supported by the Whig leaders, could only remonstrate with her upon her Tory predilections. Remonstrances having no effect, they seized with alacrity upon the famous Gregg Scandal, which proved that Harley had conducted his business as Secretary of State with great negligence, and that the clerk Gregg, who had been arrested on December 30th, 1707, had given information to the French ministers. Supported by the Whigs, Marlborough and Godolphin insisted on Harley's dismissal.

On February the 10th Harley resigned, and was followed by Simon Harcourt the Attorney-General, Mansell, and St. John. There is no difficulty in explaining St. John's resignation. His close connection with Harley, coupled with the complete ascendancy of the Whigs, to whom he could not fail to be an object of suspicion, sufficiently accounts for his action. He resigned, carrying with him the reputation of being a brilliant and successful Secretary-at-War. Marlborough had found him a most useful colleague, and in a letter to St. John in October, 1709, he expresses a hope that he may begin to entertain more favourable thoughts of the world in which he " is qualified to do so much good." He had clearly demonstrated that he was the ablest man in the Tory ranks. During his tenure of office, the English had won victories which have made the reign of Queen Anne rival even that of Elizabeth in splendour.

The objects of England in the war had been plain and straightforward, such as commended themselves to all moderate men. It was only at the end of 1707 (December 22nd) that the Whigs had boastfully and imprudently expressed the opinion that no Bourbon should be permitted to rule in Spain, and had passed a resolution that no peace would be safe or honourable if Spain, the West Indies, or any part of the Spanish monarchy was suffered to remain under the power of the House of Bourbon. It was well, then, that St. John should retire before he became closely associated with a policy which was doomed to failure. He was succeeded as Secretary-at-War by the rising politician, Robert Walpole, who had already secured the full confidence of the Whig party.

Parliament was dissolved in April, 1708, and at the new

elections the nation declared itself strongly in favour of the Whigs. An attempted Jacobite invasion of Scotland in the spring had not only found the English Government unprepared, but had clearly demonstrated the universal hatred with which the English nation was regarded in Scotland. The Jacobite chances of success were never so good as in 1708. It was natural, therefore, that all advocates of the Union should regard with alarm the possibility of the return to office of Tories like Rochester, Nottingham, and Haversham, who had protested against the Union. The firm establishment of a united Whig administration meant the resolute maintenance of the Union and the active prosecution of the war.

St. John did not seek re-election. He retired to his country house at Bucklersbury, which had belonged to his father-in-law, who had died in the previous year. It was situated in Berkshire, about twenty-five miles from Windsor and from Newbury; formerly belonging to the Reading Abbey, it had been granted after the Reformation to the son of Jack of Newbury. There, for two years, St. John devoted himself to the study of philosophy and literature. The reasons for St. John's retirement from politics are not difficult to fathom. Prudential motives, no doubt, played a considerable part in his decision. His interests and those of Harley were closely identified. Marlborough and Godolphin had succeeded in forming a united Whig administration, which included the great names of Somers, Cowper, Orford, Halifax, and Sunderland, but in so doing had lost the affection and esteem of the Queen. They had definitely broken with the moderate Tories. It was impossible for St. John to continue to act as Secretary-at-War without throwing in his lot with the Whigs. Then, again, as long as the nation was satisfied with the continuance of the war and was still intent on the annihilation of the power of France, it was useless to continue to oppose the Whigs in Parliament.   It was better to watch events from outside.   His obligations to Marlborough must also have largely influenced his decision.   To Marlborough he owed his appointment as Secretary-at-War; with Marlborough he had, during his tenure of office, been on the closest and most confidential terms.   Marlborough's power and influence showed no signs of diminution.   In July, 1708, Marlborough won the battle of Oudenarde, and St. John wrote at once from London to congratulate the great general.   At the end of the letter he says:

"The death of a grandfather" (Sir Walter St. John died at Battersea, in 1708, at the ripe age of eighty-seven) "brought me to this place, from whence I am preparing to return again to the country, in the midst of which retreat I shall inviolably preserve in my heart that gratitude for all your favours, that zeal for your service, and that true, unaffected love for your person which I have never knowingly departed from.

"I am, with the greatest respect, my Lord, etc.,

"H. St. John."

To the astonishment of his friends and acquaintances, the gay, worldly St. John, who by his wonderful oratory and riotous life had become one of the best known men in London, thus calmly withdrew from public life, and devoted himself to quiet studies in his country retreat.   He always looked back on these two years of retirement at Bucklers-bury with the greatest satisfaction.   In his letter to Lord Bathurst on *The True Use of Retirement and Study*, written many years later, he speaks of his love of study and his desire of knowledge:

"This love and this desire I have felt all my life, and I am not quite a stranger to this industry and application.   There has been something always ready to whisper in my ear while I ran the course of pleasure and of business, 'Solve senescentem mature sanus equum.'   But my genius, unlike the demon of Socrates, whispered so softly that very often I heard him not, in the hurry of those passions by which I was transported.   Some calmer hours there were; in them I hearkened to him.   Reflection had often its turn, and the love of study and the desire of knowledge have never quite abandoned me."   And he continues: "When we have secured

the necessaries, there may be time to amuse ourselves with the super-
fluities and even with the trifles of life. ' Dulce est desipere,' said
Horace ; ' Vive la bagatelle !' says Swift. I oppose neither ; not the
Epicurean, much less the Christian philosopher ; but I insist that a
principal part of these amusements be the amusements of study and reflection, of reading and conversation."

Study, reflection, reading, and conversation occupied the
two years of St. John's enforced absence from the political
struggles in Parliament.

During his retirement, Louis XIV. made at the Hague,
in 1709, a very determined effort to procure peace. In his
later writings St. John strongly insists that peace should
certainly have been made between July, 1708, and the spring
of 1709.

"It was high time indeed to save our country from absolute insolvency
and bankruptcy by putting an end to a scheme of conduct which the prejudices of a party, the whims of some particular men, the private interest
of more, and the avarice and ambition of our allies . . . alone maintained."

But the chiefs of the Whig party were determined that
no peace should be made till they had secured what they
considered to be a complete triumph over Louis XIV. As
a complete triumph meant in their eyes not only the expulsion of Philip from Spain, but his expulsion at the hands of
his grandfather, it is a matter of little wonder that Louis
preferred to carry on the war. The war had become unjust
and unnecessary. In September, 1709, Malplaquet was
won, and the bond between the Maritime Powers was
tightened by the conclusion on October the 29th of the
Barrier Treaty. By the terms of this treaty the supremacy
of the Dutch republic was, it is said, established in North-
Western Europe. In the spring of 1710 Louis again tried,
at the Conference of Gertruydenburg, to come to terms
with the Allies. The English Ministers were this time
more inclined to treat, and the French King was prepared
to make enormous concessions. But he refused to assist
the allies in the expulsion of Philip from Spain, the negotia-

tions broke down in June, and the war continued. The conduct of the Whigs was absolutely unjustifiable. The Archduke Charles, for whom we were ostensibly fighting, was now heir to the Austrian dominions. If he became King of Spain, the Empire of Charles V. might be revived. Philip was the chosen and adored King of the Spaniards. The conquest of Spain was impossible, and England was bearing the greater part of the expense of a war in which our Allies sought their own ends.

During these years, St. John watched the course of events, from his country seat. No sooner had a united Whig Ministry been formed, than it began to lose favour with the country. Outwardly it was strong, but, from a variety of causes, its position was gradually undermined. Anne had always disliked the Whigs, on account of their religious and political opinions. Since the resignation of Harley, she had broken with Godolphin and Marlborough, and only retained them in her service till an opportunity occurred to replace them by men she trusted. Her final quarrel with the Duchess of Marlborough, too, contributed not a little to encourage the enemies of the Whig junto, just at the time when the ranks of those enemies were, owing to St. John's advice and Harley's skill, reinforced by such prominent names as those of Somerset, Argyll, and Shrewsbury, Rochester, Harcourt, and Bromley. " You broke the party," wrote St. John to Harley, " unite it again." The influence of Somerset, Argyll, and Shrewsbury on the history of the reign was immense. Nominally Whigs, they were always opposed to the undisputed supremacy of one party. They largely contributed to the fall of the Whigs in 1710; they were the authors of the *coup d'état* at the end of Anne's reign, which ruined the Tory party.

There was no doubt that the Whigs, at the beginning of 1710, had failed to secure the confidence of the Queen, and had lost much of the support of the people. The middle class had learned to regard the war administration with disfavour. The ever-increasing burdens and the danger of a financial crisis, brought home to them the necessity of peace. It would appear from St. John's expression of his views at a much later period that he too shared the general distrust of the funding system which had been introduced at the Revolution, and that he too was as ignorant as the majority of his countrymen of the capability of the nation to bear the burden of the National Debt. "It is impossible," he says, in his *Dissertation on Parties*, "to look back without indignation at the mysterious iniquity by which this system has been matured, or horror to the consequences that may ensue from it" (Bolingbroke's Works, vol. iii. p. 296). The enormous increase in the public debt under the influence of the funding system had aroused almost universal apprehension at the very moment when the motives of the Ministers in prolonging the war were being anxiously criticized. It was thought that an honourable and profitable peace might have been made at the Hague in 1709, or at Gertruydenburg in 1710. The suspicion was gaining ground that the war was being unduly protracted for party purposes.

Marlborough, too, had temporarily lost much of his popularity by his well-known love of wealth, by the large amounts of public money absorbed by his connections, and by his demand of the Captain-Generalship for life. Men feared he might become a military dictator. "The shadow of Cromwell," says Mr. Lecky, "fell darkly across the path of Marlborough."

In London the Naturalization Act, passed early in 1709, by which foreign Protestants could be naturalized, had roused some excitement and indignation. The indignation at the appearance of a great number of Germans, mostly from the Palatinate, was due, not to social and economic causes, but to a supposed danger to the Church of

England, from their presence. These Germans, though Protestants, were not Church of England men, and they would, it was said, increase the ranks of the Nonconformists. The fanaticism of the masses was appealed to, and London became strongly anti-Whig.

It was at this very time, when public feeling was running against the Whigs, that Godolphin made his momentous and unfortunate decision to impeach Sacheverell. This celebrated clergyman had preached sermons in 1709, at Derby and at St. Paul's, in which he denounced the Whigs, attacked Godolphin and Marlborough directly, inveighed against toleration to Nonconformists, and inculcated plainly the duty of passive obedience. In spite of the wish of Somerset and Marlborough not to make a political matter of Sacheverell's sermons, the majority of the Ministers persisted in seeing in those sermons a direct impeachment of the principles of the Revolution. Entirely underrating the strength of High Church Toryism, and ignoring the immense influence of the ecclesiastical sentiment, they allowed their rage to get the better of their discretion, and determined to assert the authority of Parliament over the Church. The prosecution of Sacheverell roused a burst of enthusiasm on behalf of the Church from one end of the country to the other. The war was forgotten. Men only remembered that their religion was in danger. In the provinces the excitement was fully as strong as that shown in London. The trial ended in March, 1710, and Parliament was prorogued early in April. Taking advantage of the change of feeling in the country, Anne, on April the 13th, then removed Kent, the Lord Chamberlain, and appointed Shrewsbury in his place. The same day she presented Sacheverell with the living of St. Andrew's, Holborn. The astute Shrewsbury, who had personal grievances against the Whigs, had for some time past carried on secret intrigues with Harley. His unerring political instinct always led him to espouse the winning cause, and his acceptance of office on April the 13th proved to be the first step in the downfall of the Whig Ministry. In June, at Harley's suggestion, the unpopular Sunderland was dismissed from office, and Dartmouth, a moderate Tory, received his appointment. In August, Anne, at the instigation of her Tory advisers, who now had ascertained that the nation had turned against the Whigs, and that, come what might, there was no fear of Marlborough's resignation, dismissed Godolphin; with his fall, one of the most famous Ministries of the annals of English history came to an end.

With the Sacheverell Trial Harley's intrigues with Anne had undoubtedly assumed grave importance. Scribe's "Un Verre d'Eau" gives an interesting, though unhistorical and exaggerated account of the influence of a court intrigue upon the fate of Europe. There is little evidence that St. John took any part in this intrigue. At the end of 1709 there is a letter of the Duchess of Marlborough to Anne, in which that jealous and lynx-eyed lady shows that she suspected the existence of some conspiracy.

"And who are those," she writes, "that you told me you had somewhere but a few inconsiderable men, that have undertaken to carry Mrs. Masham up to a pitch of greatness, from which she would be thrown down with infamy in a fortnight? What did some people in your service ride lately about from her to Mr. Harley at London, and thence to Mr. St. John's in the country, and then back again to her, and so again to London, as if they rid post all the while, but about some notable scheme, which, I dare swear, would make the world very merry if it were known?"

St. John, no doubt, at this time, just as in 1707, was fully aware of the private colloquies of Harley with the Queen. That he was in their confidence is unlikely. Neither Anne nor Harley had any wish to make a clean sweep of the Whigs from the administration. A combination of moderate men chosen from both parties, and forming "a new party, which should look to the sovereign in person as its chief," would have suited their views admirably. St. John had so far shown no sympathy with Harley's elaborate scheme for forming a mixed administration, and Harley had certainly shown no intention of giving St. John a prominent position in the Ministry which he had designed. Harley at first, with the entire concurrence of Anne, and in accordance with his invariable views, attempted to form a Coalition Ministry, including some of the principal Whigs. If Cowper and Walpole would retain their offices, he was ready to give St. John and Harcourt only subordinate places. But, in his hour of triumph, Harley found that all his hopes of forming an ideal administration composed of men of both parties were dashed to the ground. The Whigs refused to join him, or to entertain any idea of a compromise. He was compelled to throw himself entirely on the Tories, and between August and November a Tory Government was formed, with Harley as virtual Prime Minister and Chancellor of the Exchequer; the other members being Poullett, Chief Commissioner of the Treasury and Chancellor of the Exchequer, June, 1711 to November, 1713; Rochester, President of the Council; Harcourt, Lord Keeper; Ormonde, Lord-Lieutenant of Ireland; Newcastle (a Whig), Privy Seal (succeeded in April, 1711, by Robinson, Bishop of Bristol); Dartmouth and St. John, Secretaries of State respectively for the Southern and Northern Departments; Walpole, Treasurer of the Navy till January, 1711; and Sir John Leake, First Lord of the Admiralty.

CHAPTER III

BOLINGBROKE'S DIPLOMACY : THE PEACE OF UTRECHT, 1710-1713.

Party spirit runs high—St. John's elevation to the post of Secretary of State—Feelings of the Tory party—The elections of 1710—Tory foreign policy—Peace necessary—Difficulties in the way of peace—The *Examiner*—Number Ten—Employment of Swift—Violence of the Tory squires—The October Club—Discontent at Harley's indecision—Guiscard's attack on Harley—Its effect—Harley becomes Earl of Oxford—Growing rivalry between Oxford and St. John—England's true relation to the Allies considered—Negotiations opened with France—Death of Joseph I., April, 1711—Failure of St. John's expedition to North America—Arrival of Mesnager—Preliminary articles signed in September—Discovery by the Allies of England's intention to make peace—General excitement—St. John's measures—Publication of *The Conduct of the Allies*—The famous debate in the House of Lords—Defeat of the Government—Dismissal of Marlborough—Creation of Tory Peers—St. John continues his "strong remedies"—Opening of conferences at Utrecht, January 29, 1712—Protracted character of the negotiations—St. John raised to the Peerage—Visits Paris and sees Louis XIV.—Charges against Bolingbroke—Shrewsbury sent to Paris, January, 1713, to hasten the negotiations—Bolingbroke's ultimatum—The treaties signed—Criticism of the Peace of Utrecht, of the means by which it was brought about, and of its terms—The greatness of Bolingbroke's work—He anticipated the policy of Chatham—Place occupied in English and French history by the Peace of Utrecht.

THE history of the last four years of the reign of Anne has yet to be written. Swift was too involved in the politics of the time to write more than a party pamphlet, full of inaccuracies, and partial from beginning to end. St. John himself, after his return from exile, seriously meditated writing a history of Anne's reign, and sketched a general plan of the proposed work. Unfortunately this idea was never carried out, and his seventh and eighth *Letters on History* remain as an introduction to the greater work. At no previous or succeeding period has the English nation worked itself into such a pitch of excitement ; at no other period have such momentous questions awaited decision. Never before or since have antagonisms been keener or more bitter. Neither the strong party feelings engendered by the course of the French Revolution, nor the antagonisms caused in late years by the Irish question, are to be compared to the tremendous issues which divided the Whigs and Tories in the four last years of Queen Anne's reign. Party spirit ran as high in London as in Florence or Verona in the Middle Ages. When one reads how the Tory gentlemen thirsted for the blood of the late Whig Ministers, and how, on the accession of George, the exultant Whigs clamoured for revenge on the authors of the Peace of Utrecht, one is irresistibly reminded of the feuds of the Bianchi and Neri, or of the rivalries of Capulet and Montague. The Whig and Tory ladies sat on different sides of the opera ; they carried different kinds of fans ; they " patched " on different sides of the face. " They have made schisms in the play-house," wrote Swift ; " and each have their particular sides at the opera ; and, when a man changes his party, he must invariably count upon the loss of his mistress." Old friendships which had existed for years were broken. Swift and Addison became ordinary acquaintances ; Prior was avoided by his old political friends ; the friendship between Marlborough and St. John came to an end.

With the exception of the younger Pitt, it is impossible to find an instance of a statesman of St. John's years being placed in so important an office at such a critical epoch in our history. He had certainly shown unexpected capacity as Secretary-at-War, but he was best known as a brilliant orator, an excellent conversationalist, a man of wit and

fashion, a hard drinker, a gay companion, a modern Alci-
biades. In spite of the Queen's personal dislike of him, he
was suddenly elevated to a position in a Government which
was called upon to administer the affairs of the country at
an unusually grave crisis. St. John, no doubt, owed his
position partly to his oratorical power, partly to his knowledge of French, partly to the lack of ability among the
Tories. In his *Letter to Sir William Wyndham* he confesses
that the Tories came into office at that crisis with no very
high notion of public duty :

> "I am afraid that we came to Court in the same disposition as all
> parties have done ; that the principal spring of our actions was to have the
> government of the State in our hands ; that our principal views were the
> conservation of this power, great employment to ourselves, and great
> opportunities of rewarding those who had helped to raise us, and of hurting
> those who stood in opposition to us. It is, however, true that with these
> considerations of private and party interest there were others intermingled
> which had for their object the public good of the nation—at least, what
> we took to be such."

Parliament was dissolved in September, 1710. The result
of the elections was to give the Tories a strong majority in
the Commons. St. John was returned for Berkshire.
William Bromley, the Tory member of Oxford University,
was elected Speaker, and on the same day Atterbury was
chosen Prolocutor of Convocation—elections which typified
the close connection between the Government and the
Church. In spite, however, of the overthrow of the Whigs,
the Government was from the first in a far from secure position. A general panic had seized the nation that the Whig
Ministers were bent on overthrowing the Church. The
conviction that all Whigs were Republicans, Atheists, or
Nonconformists, was widespread. It was believed that the
continuance of the Whigs in office meant the downfall of
the Church in England. Religious feeling had been violently stirred up. For the time, the French war had been
forgotten, and the great Whig Ministry had been prevented,

in a moment of frenzy, from carrying on and concluding the war which it had hitherto successfully waged. It was obvious a reaction would ere long set in—a reaction danger-ous to the new Ministers, if they had not in the interval proved themselves worthy of confidence. Even at the time of the Sacheverell trial the Tory leaders feared that if Marl-borough resigned the nation might suddenly return to its senses. As soon as Godolphin's dismissal was known, the commercial classes had shown their distrust of the change of Government; a panic had taken place in the City, and the Bank shares fell from 140 to 110. Unless the Ministers could gain the confidence of the "moneyed" classes, it would be impossible to raise the enormous loans which were absolutely necessary. Then, again, the large Tory majority was itself a difficulty to Harley and the moderate section of the Tories, who had desired a mixed administration, in which the Tory element should merely preponderate. They found themselves in the hands of men like St. John and Harcourt, who, supported by the country members full of animosity towards Nonconformists, and the "moneyed" class, were for no half measure. But the Tory squires, half unconsciously, no doubt, were only endeavouring to carry out a line of policy which, though ultimately unsuccessful, was, nevertheless, a distinct policy. The Revolution had destroyed the predominance of the Church and of the landed interest in the Government. The object of the Tories was to restore that predominance. To defend the Church from the encroachments of Nonconformists, to vest the Govern-ment of the country in the hands of the landed gentry, to recognize as far as possible hereditary right in the succes-sion—these were the principles which Queen Anne's Ministers, from 1710 to 1714, attempted to assert.

"We looked," wrote St. John in after-years, "on the political prin-ciples which had generally prevailed in our Government from the Revolu-tion of 1688 to be destructive to our true interest, to have mingled us too much in the affairs of the Continent to tend to the impoverishing our people, and to the loosening the bands of our constitution in Church and State."

Both Harley and St. John were in full agreement on the question of peace. *Peace was an absolute necessity.* As long as the war continued, Marlborough was the most powerful subject, and the Ministry remained dependent on the "moneyed interest." The continuance of the war would obviously only result in the triumphant supremacy of Marlborough and the Whigs. Besides, it was the conviction of the Ministers that :—

"the war, which had been begun for the security of the Allies, was continued for their grandeur ; that the ends proposed when we engaged in it might have been answered long before ; and therefore that the first favourable occasion ought to be seized of making peace."

In other words, considerations of foreign policy rendered the Ministers desirous to end a war with the aims of which they had no sympathy. Important questions of internal policy, too, demanded their full attention.

The questions of peace and of the succession were closely connected. The Whigs firmly believed that the existence of a free Government in England, as well as the Hanoverian succession, depended on upholding the Grand Alliance and on reducing France to the position of a second-rate power. If the Queen's death found the Whig party in power, strongly supported by the "moneyed" class and by a large army led by a successful and popular general, the Parliamentary succession would be safe. The Tories, on the other hand, disliked standing armies, and, like many people at the present day, wished to strengthen, and to rely almost entirely on the fleet for defence against external foes. So far from thinking with the Whigs that the succession of an Austrian prince to Spain was a matter of European importance, they regarded Austria as a power which already had leant on England long enough, and had pursued her own separate advantage at the expense of the allies to an extent sufficient to deprive her of any further consideration at the hands of England. Both Austria and Holland were indeed actively engaged in looking after their own territorial and commercial ends, while England, who was bearing by far the largest share of the expense, could gain but little to compensate her for the money and blood expended. The Tories, too, represented the dislike of the great mass of the people to foreign interference. To withdraw England, then, from her Continental connections, so as to enable her to deal with her own domestic affairs without any foreign interference, was the main plank in St. John's foreign policy— a policy of non-intervention. It was of the greatest possible importance that peace should be made before the death of the Queen. Each party thought the possession of power, when that event should take place, was most vital to their respective interests. The hands of Ministers must be free, so as to enable them to make terms with the successor of the Queen, and thus to secure the continuance of their party in the enjoyment of the executive power. It is well to note that St. John, in his *Letter to Sir William Wyndham*, says that at this time "there was no formed design in the party against His Majesty's accession to the throne. On the latter, and most other points, they affected a most glorious neutrality."

The Tory policy was then clear. Satisfactory terms must be forced from Louis by an active prosecution of the war, and, at the same time, the war policy of the Whigs must be rendered unpopular. The attempts of Harley and St. John to impress their views on the public mind constitute an epoch in the history of English political literature. As early as August, 1710, the *Examiner* had made its first appearance chiefly owing to the efforts of St. John in order to educate public opinion. No. 10, afterwards entitled a *Letter to The Examiner*, though written anonymously, was soon known to have come from the pen of St. John himself.

In this, St. John's first famous political production, he blames the late Ministry for neglecting to obtain at the first opportunity an honourable peace, and ends his paper by a violent denunciation of the Duchess of Marlborough, and of her tyranny over the Queen. No. 10 attracted very considerable attention and provoked several replies, of which the most celebrated was written by Cowper, who attacked the views of Harley and St. John in the *Tatler*. We have here, as Sir Walter Scott observes, " the singular picture of two statesmen, each at the head of their respective parties, condescending to become correspondents of the conductors of the periodical writings in politics."

In November, 1710, Swift, now animated by deep hostility to the Whigs, was intoduced to Harley, and began a series of celebrated articles in the *Examiner*, in which, following on the lines of No. 10, he attacked the Whigs and their policy, urged the repudiation of the National Debt, and still further undermined the popular regard for Marlborough. There is no doubt whatever that, as long as Marlborough remained in command of the army and still retained a considerable amount of popularity at home, peace was practically impossible. To destroy his influence by repeated invectives in the *Examiner* against ambition and avarice, and then to deprive him of his command, became a necessary preliminary to the conclusion of any peace between a Tory Ministry and Louis XIV. Before, however, such a step could be taken, all Harley's political skill had to be called into play, in order to educate public opinion, and place the Ministry in a sufficiently strong position. During the winter the struggle was severe, and for a time the result seemed doubtful.

Always anxious to conciliate opponents, and to rely on the moderate Tories, and if possible on the moderate Whigs, Harley had at first attempted to make an arrangement with Marlborough. Through his agent John Drummond, an

Amsterdam merchant, St. John laid down the terms which the Ministers demanded from Marlborough. He must give up his old friends and make "positive engagements to co-operate heartily in all the policy of the Tories."

Late in December, 1710, Marlborough arrived in England, and had two interviews with St. John, by whom he was soundly lectured for abandoning the Tory party. Marlborough, however, did not join the Tories, and, though he continued at the head of the army, it was obvious that his fall was only a matter of time, and Harley was forced to rely more and more on the Tory squires, then as ever strongly opposed to a policy of moderation. The disaster of Brihuega in December had given them a welcome opportunity for attacking the late Ministers. The Tories had always held, in opposition to Marlborough, that the operations in Spain ought not to be subordinate to those in Flanders. Brihuega, they asserted, proved the justice of this view. In both houses the late administration was attacked. In the House of Lords, the Whig stronghold, resolutions were passed blaming Whig ministers for the misfortunes in Spain, and complimenting Peterborough, who was now attached to the Tory leaders. In the Commons the financial administration of the Whigs was violently censured. A Bill repealing the Naturalization Act was thrown out by the Lords after it had passed the Commons. A Bill praised by Swift in the *Examiner* as "that noble Bill of Qualification," and warmly supported by St. John, compelling all Members of Parliament to possess a certain income from landed property, passed both Houses of Parliament, and a committee organized by Harley and St. John was named to inquire into the expenditure of the Whig Government. But such measures did not satisfy the Tory squires. They wanted the dismissal of the Whigs from all posts in the country as well as in London. They expected the immediate repression of Nonconformists and the establishmen of the Crown on the basis of hereditary right; they looked for impeachments and executions. The October Club, which, founded in the autumn of 1710, met at the Bell Tavern in King Street, Westminster, held nightly meetings, at which the discontented Members of Parliament inveighed against Harley's moderation, to them so incomprehensible. St. John, with his invincible eloquence, was far more to their taste than the temporizing, unintelligible Harley. The former understood the nature of the men who then composed the House of Commons. "They grow," he wrote, "like hounds, fond of the men who show them game, and by whose halloa they are used to be encouraged." His experience, too, as Secretary-at-War gave him unusual opportunities for discovering blots in the financial administration of the war. His growing popularity in the House of Commons had not escaped the notice of Harley, who now began to fear that St. John might prove a successful rival.

Apparently the Treasurer and Secretary were on the most intimate terms. With Harcourt they directed the policy of the Government, and from the end of January, 1711, they dined together every Saturday afternoon, Swift being, from February the 17th, included in the party. Just when the discontent against Harley was assuming dangerous proportions, the attack on him by Guiscard, a French spy, restored his popularity, and strengthened the position of the Ministry. During St. John's first tenure of office, he and Guiscard had been boon companions. Godolphin had aided him to form a regiment of refugees which was to land in France and create a diversion in the interest of the Allies. Not being properly supported by the Whigs, the regiment was disbanded, and soon after a pension which had been granted him was discontinued. On becoming Secretary of State, St. John had procured for him a pension, which Harley afterwards reduced. Furious at this treatment, the unfortunate adventurer then offered to act as a spy in England in the service of the French Government. His letters being seized, he was brought before the Council and interrogated by St. John. On being refused a private interview by the Secretary, Guiscard stabbed Harley, who was near him, in the breast with a pen-knife. St. John at once ran him through with his sword, and the unfortunate Guiscard died shortly afterwards in Newgate. Harley, who by the testimony of St. John, had behaved throughout with great firmness, at once became a martyr for religion, his country, and his Queen. His popularity was immense. The death of Rochester left him without a rival. On the 23rd of May, 1711, he was created Baron Harley of Wigmore, Earl of Oxford, and a week later Lord Treasurer. "He had grown," as Swift said, "by persecution, turning out and stabbing." At this very time the Committee employed in examining the financial administration for the late Government presented its report, which showed that upwards of thirty-five millions sterling were unaccounted for.

In June Parliament was prorogued. Thus far Oxford had guided the Government with considerable skill. Himself a moderate Tory, he had contrived to strengthen the position of his party without yielding to the extreme section of his followers. He had seen the necessity of securing able writers on the side of the Government, and he had employed Swift, Defoe, Prior, and Parnell. The "moneyed" class had begun to show confidence in the Ministry, and on the whole all was going well, though the "isthmus" on which the Ministry stood was narrow.

In the summer and autumn the Ministry was reconstructed on a firm Tory basis. In June Robert Benson became Chancellor of the Exchequer, to be succeeded in that post in November, 1713, by Sir William Wyndham. John Sheffield, First Duke of Buckinghamshire, was appointed Lord President, while Henry St. John and Dartmouth remained Secretaries of State, the latter being succeeded in

August, 1713, by William Bromley. In April John Robinson, Bishop of Bristol, had taken the office of Lord Privy
Seal, hitherto held by the Duke of Newcastle, who died in
July. This appointment had led Swift to remark that " it
will bind the Church to him (Harley) for ever." Sir John
Leake and the Duke of Ormonde continued in their offices,
the former being succeeded in 1712 by the Earl of Strafford.

From this time, however, the rivalry between St. John
and Oxford became a source of weakness to the Administration. The friendly Saturday dinners ceased soon after
Harley's elevation, and the formation in June of the Society
of Brothers, intended by St. John to be a rival, partly
literary, partly political to the Kitcat Club, failed to heal the
growing breach between the two Statesmen. But for the
time the struggle for pre-eminence in the Cabinet was deferred. It was evident that the position of the Government
would be imperilled unless peace, and a peace advantageous
to England, was not shortly made.

The advisability of peace had been debated by the
Ministers on their accession to power. " We must have
peace," Swift wrote in March in his Journal, " let it be a
good or a bad one, though nobody dares talk of it." But
the difficulties in the way of peace were enormous. As a
member of the Grand Alliance, England was bound (1) not
to treat with France, except " jointly and in concert " with
the rest of the allies, (2) to co-operate with her allies for the
attainment of certain common objects. St. John, representing the Government, laid down, early in 1711 and at various
times throughout the year, the "new footing " on which
England was prepared to act, and " the new principles "
which were to guide the foreign policy of England. Since
1706 there had ceased to be a common cause binding the
allies together ; the object of the Grand Alliance had been
accomplished ; the enormous power of France had been reduced ; France had abandoned in 1706 her claim to the

entire Spanish monarchy. After that date the war had changed its character. It was no longer just or necessary. It had become a war of ambition, of selfish interests, of plunder, of individual aggrandizement. Hence it was resolved that each Ally was to "advance and manage his own pretensions," that England was to separate her interests from those of the Allies, though not to formally withdraw from the Alliance. Having secured her own interests, she would then at a Conference join the Allies, who would be compelled to agree to the proposals which England and France had previously drawn up.

It was obvious to Oxford and St. John that this course was most perilous. The general opinion in the country was that the war was a just one, and that, after Marlborough's brilliant victories, England ought certainly to secure enormous advantages. It was uncertain, too, how their Tory supporters would view a secret arrangement with France, which, though advantageous to England, would necessarily mean serious modifications in the concessions of France to the Allies. To postpone peace would be indeed fatal to the Tory scheme of policy; to avow the means by which alone peace could be made would involve the whole party in immediate ruin. It was, therefore, determined to open secret negotiations without delay with France, and at the same time, till the negotiations had advanced a considerable step, to disclaim, if necessary, all intention of separating England's interests from those of the Allies. Dartmouth being Secretary of the Southern Department, the management of the negotiations should properly have been in his hands; but St. John's abilities, combined with his knowledge of French, rendered it absolutely necessary that, with the charge of the Northern Department, he should be practically Secretary of State for Foreign Affairs. His correspondence during these years teems in consequence with illustrations of the double-dealing, the dissimulation, the trickery necessary to carry through a policy which involved so much intrigue. In the Queen's Speech at the opening of Parliament at the end of November, 1710, the vigorous prosecution of the war, especially in Spain, was recommended, and for a time the Tories were compelled to appear as zealous for war as their opponents. None the less were the Ministers determined to carry out their peace policy without delay. In January, 1711, Gaultier, a French priest, well known to Lord Jersey, St. John's relative, was sent to inform Torcy, the chief Minister in France, verbally, that the English Government desired peace. In Gaultier the Ministers reposed the greatest confidence. " From first to last," wrote Bolingbroke in later days, " Gaultier has been in the whole secret of every transaction relating to the peace." While Marlborough was carrying on a campaign in the Netherlands, Gaultier was sent a second time to ask the French Minister for some definite proposals. Louis was now in a stronger position. The Allies, after the disasters of Brihuega and Villa Viciosa, only held Catalonia. Louis' tone, therefore, was very different from what it had been at the Conferences at the Hague or at Gertruydenburg. Still, at the end of April, Gaultier returned with technically " the first overture " from the French Government. On April the 27th St. John sent a copy of the French overture to Lord Raby, our Ambassador at the Hague, telling him to communicate it to the Grand Pensionary Heinsius, and to beg him to keep the matter secret.

The death of the Emperor Joseph in April, 1711, strengthened the hands of the Tories. It was clear to them that to revive the Empire of Charles V. in the person of the Archduke Charles would be more disadvantageous to the balance of power than to allow Philip to remain in possession of Spain.

From May to the middle of July the negotiations between England and France were suspended, owing to the endeavours—foreseen by St. John—of the Dutch to secure separate terms from the French. In May St. John made his well-known attempt to gain popularity for the Ministry by an expedition, the object of which was the expulsion of the French from Canada and the capture of Newfoundland. In this deliberate attack upon the French power in the New World, St. John anticipated the policy of Chatham. Had the expedition been successful, the effect would have been very great upon the negotiations. In July the negotiations were resumed, and it was then thought advisable to associate with Gaultier some trustworthy agent who should act as the English plenipotentiary. For this post, Prior, who had been Secretary to the British Legation in Paris at the close of William III.'s reign and since the beginning of the war a Commissioner of Trade, was chosen. With the exception of the short periods when Bolingbroke and Shrewsbury were in Paris, Prior was in full charge of the negotiations, though, as a matter of fact, his powers were extremely limited. His principal duty was to receive the answers of Louis XIV. to the demands of the English Ministers. In the middle of July, Prior and Gaultier, under fictitious names, made their way to Paris, the former bearing a long list of England's preliminary demands, and in the early days of August shortly after St. John had written a letter congratulating Marlborough upon his strategic success near Bouchain, they returned with Mesnager, a Rouen merchant, to whom the French King had intrusted the duty of discussing the proposed terms of peace and of drawing up preliminary articles.

On the 7th of September, eight preliminary articles were signed by St. John and Dartmouth on behalf of England, by Mesnager on behalf of France and Spain. During the progress of the negotiations it was obvious to Mesnager that the life of the Ministry depended upon securing advantageous terms. When all the other Ministers showed signs of tre-

pidation, Shrewsbury being especially agitated and anxious,
St. John alone was firm and resolute.

His determination to carry through the peace is further
evidenced by a letter to Drummond on September the 4th,
in which he says that the Queen's Ministers

> " will depend on the course and tenor of their proceedings, to set their
> merit in a just and proper light, without being frightened, vexed, or
> diverted from their measures by any suspicions which may be entertained
> of them, or by any clamour which may be raised against them."

As soon as Mesnager, whose residence in England had
been a profound secret, was safe in France, a set of preliminary articles different from those drawn up between
England and France, and which included a Barrier for the
Dutch, were formally communicated to the Allied Powers.

In the middle of October, Gallas, the Imperial Ambassador, whose fury at the evident determination of the
English Ministers to end the war knew no bounds, and
who, "with the natural impertinence of a German, improved by conversation with a saucy English faction,"
styled England's policy as an "enigma," and sent a copy
of these articles to the *Daily Courant.* The country, which
was unaware that England's interests had been carefully
considered in a separate and secret agreement, was in a fer-
ment ; the friendship between St. John and Marlborough
came to an end, and the latter returned to England in
November, the declared enemy of the Tories. Buys, the
self-opinionated Pensionary of Amsterdam, had been already
sent from Holland to remonstrate, and his house became
the headquarters of the Opposition. There the Whigs met
the foreign Envoys. There was composed a memorial presented by Bothmar, the Hanoverian envoy, in which a
gloomy picture was drawn of the danger to England's
independence from the policy of the Government. On
November the 17th serious disturbances were expected,
and the trained bands of London and Westminster were

called out. Somerset soon after avowed himself hostile to the Ministerial policy, and this was the more serious, since his wife at that time stood high in Anne's affections.

The general opinion still was that, though peace would be desirable, the French King should be forced to give up Spain. The real meaning of the death of Joseph in April and its effect on the course of the war seems to have been unperceived by all save the Tory statesmen. Numerous pamphlets appeared, attacking the Ministers. Even Nottingham, the high Tory Churchman, made through the medium of Somerset a compact with the Whigs, disgraceful to all parties, according to which the Whigs were to allow the Occasional Conformity Bill to pass, on consideration of his aid in censuring the preliminary articles. Immediate action was necessary. The enemies of the Government must be attacked and defeated; the negotiations must be proceeded with without delay; a public opinion in favour of peace must be formed.

"When I undertook," wrote Bolingbroke later, with reference to this crisis, "in opposition to all the confederates, in opposition to a powerful turbulent faction at home, in opposition even to those habits of thinking which mankind had contracted by the same wrong principle of Government pursued for twenty years, to make a peace, the utmost vigour and resolution became necessary."

And he led the attack on the Whigs by severe measures against the pamphleteers.

Writing to the Queen on October the 17th, he says: "I have discovered the author of another scandalous libel, who will be in custody this afternoon; he will make the thirteenth I have seized, and the fifteenth I have found out."

In all, fourteen booksellers and printers were arrested and warned; Gallas was ordered to leave the country. The Earl of Strafford (formerly Lord Raby) was at once sent to Holland with St. John's instructions to combine persuasion and firmness in the difficult task of reconciling the Dutch to the published articles. The meeting of Parliament was deferred till Swift's *Conduct of the Allies* had appeared. During the summer Oxford and St. John were accustomed to spend alternate Sundays at Windsor. There, in a small house lent to St. John, Swift and the Secretary of State often met, and there *The Conduct of the Allies* was in great measure written under St. John's direction. It is consequently to be regarded rather as a State paper than as a mere party pamphlet, especially as Oxford revised it, and made many suggestions. The object of this celebrated work was to educate the people, and to convert them from the Whig view that no peace would be safe or honourable without the restitution by the Bourbons of the whole of the Spanish dominions. It exposed Marlborough's rapacity, and dealt what amounted to a death-blow to his already declining popularity. It showed that England should have acted in the war as an auxiliary, not as a principal; that the Allies had failed to carry out their engagements; and that nearly the whole burden of maintaining the struggle had devolved upon England, who, moreover, was prevented by the Allies from recompensing herself by conquests in the West Indies. This pamphlet appeared on November the 27th, just before Parliament met, and its effect was extraordinary. Eleven thousand copies were sold before the end of January, and there is no doubt that it influenced the opinions of the great body of Englishmen strongly in favour of peace.

At last, on December the 7th, Parliament met, and Nottingham moved, as an amendment to the Address that "No peace could be safe or honourable if Spain and the West Indies were allotted to any branch of the House of Bourbon."

He was supported by Marlborough, who in a dignified speech expressed the Whig hatred of the House of Bourbon. By the Whigs—nay, by most Englishmen—Louis XIV. was regarded as a tyrant, whose ambition threatened all

Europe, especially all Protestant Europe. To their excited imaginations, the danger of allowing Spain and France to be governed by Bourbon Princes hardly required demonstration. Nottingham's amendment was carried by sixty-one against fifty-five.

The month of December was an anxious time for the Ministers. The Queen had allowed Somerset to escort her to her carriage after the debate, and Somerset had voted against the Government. The Duchess of Somerset was supposed to have supplanted Mrs. Masham in the favour of the Queen. In the House of Lords, the Whigs, after allowing—in accordance with their compact with Nottingham—the Occasional Conformity Bill to pass, had secured another victory over the Tories by refusing to allow the Duke of Hamilton to sit as an English Peer (as Duke of Brandon). Things looked black for the Government. Swift was in despair, and asked St. John for some foreign mission, so that he might be out of danger in the hour of the Whig triumph. St. John, who was especially attacked by Nottingham's motion, laughed at Swift's fears, and assured him that there was no danger. But it was time for the Ministers to act, and when so much depended on peace being made without delay, and when failure meant ruin, a man of St. John's firm yet impetuous temperament could not hesitate. Oxford himself was roused, and a series of blows were aimed at the Whigs which bore down all opposition. In the *London Gazette* of January the 1st, 1712, it was announced that twelve new Peers had been created, and that Marlborough had been dismissed from all his employments. St. John is reputed to have said: " If these twelve had not been enough, we would have given them another dozen "; but afterwards, when exile had given time for reflection, he spoke of the creation of the twelve peers " as an unprecedented invidious measure, to be excused by nothing but the necessity, and hardly by that."

During this important session St. John was the acknowledged leader of the Tories in the House of Commons,
where he had an immense majority. In February, 1712,
Swift wrote to Stella that "The Secretary is much the
greatest Commoner in England, and turns the whole Parliament, who can do nothing without him, and, if he lives
and has health, will, I believe, be one day at the head of
affairs." During the ensuing session St. John continued
the "strong remedies." Resolutions were passed, declaring
Marlborough guilty of illegal practices in the Netherlands
and liable for half a million of money. "The Duke of
Marlborough's friends," wrote St. John to Strafford, "may
be as industrious as they please on your side of the water,
and on ours too, but he has sunk himself beyond redemp-
tion." Walpole had already been imprisoned in the Tower
"on a vexatious charge of venality in the Navy Office."
All criticisms of the Government policy were checked with
a heavy hand. A Whig member who ventured to call in
question the action of the Ministers was threatened by
St. John with imprisonment, and in April a Stamp Duty
was imposed for the purpose of repressing libels. To impress still more on the public mind the wisdom of the Tory
peace policy, a Parliamentary Representation was drawn
up, which embodied several resolutions, blaming the Emperor and the Dutch for not having fulfilled their obligations, and censuring the Barrier Treaty, which, signed by
Townshend in 1709, would, if executed, have placed the
entire Netherlands with all its wealth in the hands of the
Dutch. The *Conduct of the Allies*, published in the previous
November, and followed up in December by Swift's *Remark on the Barrier Treaty*, had had a profound effect. The
subordination of English interests to those of the Allies
under the Whig administration, and the rapacity and selfishness of the Allies themselves were now well known. Marlborough had been an obstacle in the way of peace. His

dismissal had not only removed the chief danger to the
Ministry but had caused a rise in the Stocks, and the
"moneyed" interest now looked keenly for a Treaty containing terms favourable to England.

This bold and audacious line of policy, so thoroughly
characteristic of St. John, was successful. Ministers were
enabled to devote all their attention to the negotiations for
peace, which, in spite of Eugene's visit to England early in
the year, had been opened at Utrecht on January the 29th,
1712. During the next fifteen months St. John had the
difficult task of negotiating a Treaty which should satisfy
the nation. To the protracted character of these negotiations was in great measure due the ultimate failure of
St. John's attempt to place the Tory party on a stable basis.
From the year 1711 down to the conclusion of peace, there
were always two sets of negotiations proceeding ; an open
negotiation carried on in conjunction with the European
powers, and a secret correspondence between the English
and French Ministers, the object of which was to arrange
terms of peace satisfactory to England and France, and
then to force them upon the rest of the Allies. The French
Minister was kept regularly informed of the policy of the
English Government, of their instructions to Strafford, of
the communications of the Allied ambassadors, and of the
plans of the Whigs.

The Conference at Utrecht opened with considerable
bitterness. The Austrians and Dutch were furious on
realizing that England no longer intended to continue a
war for their benefit. Encouraged by the divisions among
the Allies and by the policy of England, the French at once
took a high tone, for which the English public was entirely
unprepared. The attitude of Louis and the proposals he
made roused a deep feeling of indignation in England. It
was evident that peace on the French terms would never
be accepted. The English Ministers accordingly sent

Oxford's cousin to Utrecht with fresh instructions. It is impossible not to admire the determined attitude taken up by St. John. He was more than ever resolved to force on without delay a peace which should satisfy the English expectations. " The French will see," he wrote to Strafford, " that there is a possibility of reviving the love of war in our people, by the indignation which has been expressed at the plan given in at Utrecht."

The death of the Duke of Burgundy in February, in his thirtieth year, presented a fresh difficulty. A sickly infant —afterwards Louis XV.— alone stood between the succession of Philip of Spain to France. The alarm of Europe at the probable early union of the French and Spanish crowns was general. St. John, however, was ready with a plan. Philip was offered the alternative of abdicating in favour of the Duke of Savoy, and continuing to enjoy his rights as heir-presumptive of France, or of being recognized as King of Spain, after renouncing for himself and his heirs the crown of France.

Till Philip's answer was received, the negotiations at Utrecht were naturally at a standstill. The Allies had never ceased warlike preparations, hoping to secure by some military success their ascendancy at the Conference, and so to force better terms from Louis. It was obvious that English Ministers, bound as they were by secret engagements to France, could not allow the English troops to take any part in actual hostilities. In May St. John sent a despatch to Ormonde, who commanded the forces, ordering him " to avoid engaging in any siege or hazarding a battle." The rage of the Allies and of the Whigs in England was intense. In St. John's opinion, expressed in after-years, this step was justifiable in every respect. It might indeed be argued that the Allies had no right to complain. Had not the Emperor, without consulting the Allies, made the Pacification of Milan, thus setting free French veterans who turned the scale against us in Spain at Almanza? Had he not, without consulting the rest of the Allies, sent 12,000 troops to conquer Naples for himself, when he ought to have aided the attack on Toulon? Then the Dutch had no right to complain. Again and again they had hampered Marlborough and defeated his designs. In 1703, and again in 1705, the action of the Dutch had tied his hands. Had not, too, both the Emperor and the Dutch failed most singularly to contribute their share of the stipulated expenses? Nothing could check the powerful will of St. John, supported by the general feeling of weariness of the war. In June the Whigs made their last attempt to put obstacles in the way of peace. In the same month a suspension of arms for two months was openly declared between England and France, and the British forces were withdrawn from acting in concert with the Allies. The Rubicon had been passed. On the 4th of July St. John was raised to the Peerage with the title of Baron St. John of Lydiard Tregoze, and Viscount Bolingbroke. He had expected an earldom, and he attributed his disappointment to the jealousy of Oxford. Certain it is that from henceforth the hatred felt by Bolingbroke for his leader was unmistakable, and the feud between them became impossible to be healed.

A temporary rupture of the negotiations caused by the rage of the Allies at the action of England and by a quarrel between the Dutch and French envoys did not disconcert Bolingbroke. His impatience at each fresh check to the conclusion of peace determined him if necessary to make a separate treaty with France. As negotiations by writing consumed too much valuable time, he decided to visit the Minister Torcy in Paris, and early in August, accompanied by Prior, he carried out his resolution.

On the Saturday after his arrival, Bolingbroke had an interview with Louis XIV. at Fontainebleau. That aged monarch, who spoke rapidly and indistinctly, expressed his desire for peace, and his respect for the Queen of England. The general wish for peace and the reception given him by the King secured to Bolingbroke the most enthusiastic reception in Paris. On entering the theatre as the *Cid* was being performed, the whole house rose to receive him, and several times during the evening manifested their respect for the illustrious statesman.

Ten days' personal interview with Torcy smoothed many difficulties, and on his return to London a tuspension of arms for four months was proclaimed, and was received with signs of universal joy.

It was during his stay in Paris that Azzurini Conti, the Jacobite spy, asserted that Bolingbroke had two private interviews with the Pretender. The truth of this assertion has been questioned, and, in the absence of more reliable evidence, it seems unlikely that such interviews took place. Azzurini's character is not such as to inspire confidence in his statements. On his arrival in England in April, 1711, he wormed himself into the confidence of the Jacobites, and betrayed their secrets to Heinsius, Bothmar, and Zinzendorf, the Imperial Ambassador at the Hague. Strafford discovered his practices, and informed Bolingbroke, with the satisfactory result that Azzurini's son, who was also implicated, was enticed to Paris, and imprisoned in the Bastille, where he remained till 1726. The elder Azzurini, who had returned to Italy, was arrested later and imprisoned. The tendency of the Azzurini family to mendacity makes it impossible to accept as true such isolated statements as the above. There seems, however, no doubt that Bolingbroke and the Chevalier were at the Opera on the same night. Bolingbroke himself owned to Swift that he saw the Pretender once at Paris. " He protested to me," wrote Swift to Archbishop King in 1716, " that he never saw him but once, and that was at a great distance in public, at the Opera." This incident naturally was seized upon by "les bien intentionnés " (as the Jacobites called themselves) as a hopeful sign, and many were the speculations to which it gave rise.

He was also accused of having been betrayed into some official indiscretions, which, if true, were more serious. In order to discover the extent of Bolingbroke's powers, Torcy had determined to employ a certain well-known Madame de Tencin, and her married sister, Madame de Ferriole. Madame de Tencin, after renouncing her vows as a nun, had settled in Paris with her brother, the Abbé de Tencin, a most worthless character, afterwards secretary to the Duke of Orleans. Bolingbroke contracted a close intimacy with these people, and in 1808 three volumes of letters were published in France, mainly consisting of letters between Bolingbroke and Madame de Ferriole, between 1712 and 1736, and between Bolingbroke and the Abbé Alari between 1718 and 1736. By means of these sisters, Torcy, it was said, gained the desired information, and, as if to heap coals of fire on the heads of the Tencins, Bolingbroke, so far unconscious of the treachery to which he had been subject, shortly afterwards used his influence with Victor Amadeus to secure to the Abbé de Tencin an abbey in Savoy, which had been presented to him by Louis XIV. during the period in which that province was in French hands. It was in consequence of these widely exaggerated, if not absolutely unfounded rumours about this conduct in Paris that Oxford rashly allowed his personal feelings to get the better of his discretion, and tried for a short time to carry on the foreign negotiations without Bolingbroke's assistance. It was soon seen that he was indispensable, and, after a short interval, he resumed his former duties.

His difficulties at this trying time were tremendous. So serious became the dissensions between himself and Oxford, especially after the latter had passed him over in the disposal of Godolphin's Order of the Garter, that he retired to

Bucklersbury for a fortnight, and all the efforts of Swift only succeeded in patching up the quarrel. Further delays also occurred in the course of the negotiations. Oxford and the other members of the Cabinet were by no means in entire agreement with regard to the terms of Bolingbroke's understanding with Torcy. In November, too, the Duke of Hamilton, who was on the point of starting to Paris as the English Envoy, was killed in a duel, and great difficulty was experienced in finding a suitable successor. At length the Duke of Shrewsbury was appointed. It was, however, not till January, 1713, that he started, the special object of his mission being to try and make satisfactory arrangements with regard to the cession of Newfoundland and Nova Scotia, and to conclude a commercial treaty on which Bolingbroke had set his heart. The private negotiations between England and France, and the public negotiations at Utrecht, which had been resumed in October, dragged on slowly through the winter of 1712-13. It was impossible for the Ministers to meet Parliament till they could lay before both Houses the Treaties of Peace. Bolingbroke's letters to Prior mark the sense of danger felt by the Ministers should the negotiations end in failure.

" To you," he wrote, " I can only add that we stand on the brink of a precipice, but the French stand there too. Pray tell M. de Torcy from me, that he may get Robin and Harry (Oxford and Bolingbroke) hanged, but affairs will soon run backward into so much confusion that he will wish us alive again."

In February, 1713, Bolingbroke sent an ultimatum to Shrewsbury for the French Court, and on March the 19th he wrote to Strafford that :—

" the long suspense of the Treaty gives hopes to their faction, and consequently increases their clamour and whets their rage ; whilst those who wish well to their country, and who are a vast majority in every part of the kingdom, grow tired with expectation, and uneasy under the delay."

The result of the firm attitude and determined perseverance of Bolingbroke, aided by the efforts of Prior and

5

Shrewsbury in France, and of Drummond and Strafford in Holland, was that on the 31st of March the Treaties of Utrecht were signed.

On the 9th of April Parliament met, and the Queen in her Speech informed the Houses that the Treaties were now signed, and that measures had been taken for securing the Protestant Succession. The successful conclusion of the war only roused the Whigs to fresh exertions, and no better illustration can be found of the height to which party feeling ran, than the scene at Covent Garden, where Addison's *Cato* was brought out.

The Whigs attempted to see in *Cato* a representation of Marlborough lamenting the expiring liberties of his country, but Bolingbroke cleverly turned the tables on his opponents by presenting the leading actor, Booth, with fifty guineas for defending the cause of liberty so well against a perpetual dictator.

On the 5th of May, 1713, peace was proclaimed in London, and was received with universal rejoicing.

The Peace of Utrecht is Bolingbroke's best known achievement. His reputation as a statesman is closely bound up with it ; and no judgment of his character and abilities would be complete without a careful consideration of the necessity of the Peace, and of the means by which it was brought about. Its conclusion marks the overthrow of that Whig foreign policy which aimed at establishing great Continental alliances, to uphold and support the Parliamentary Settlement. According to the Whig view, France, the ally of the Pretender, was England's enemy, and therefore should be deprived of all means of endangering England's liberty and independence. By the Peace of Utrecht the foreign guarantees of the Parliamentary Settlement were now in great part destroyed, and the Tory policy of freeing England from her Continental connections was triumphant. There is no doubt that peace was necessary and expedient. The death of the Emperor Joseph in 1711 made it impossible for English statesmen to labour for the revival of the Empire of Charles V. England too had nothing to gain by the continuance of the war. She had borne by far the largest part of the expense, and the war had cost her fifty-three millions. Bolingbroke, in a letter to Lord Raby on May the 6th, 1711, sums up admirably some of the reasons for making peace without delay :—

"We are now in the tenth campaign of a war, the great load of which has fallen on Britain, as the great advantage of it is proposed to redound to the House of Austria and to the States-General. They are in interest more immediately, we more remotely, concerned. However, what by our forwardness to engage in every article of expense, what by our private assurances, and what by our public Parliamentary declarations, that no peace should be made without the entire restitution of the Spanish monarchy, we are become principals in the contest ; the war is looked upon as our war, and it is treated accordingly by the confederates, even by the Imperialists and by the Dutch. . . .

". . . On the other hand, our Allies have always looked first at home, and the common cause has been served by the best of them in the second place. From hence it is that our commerce has been neglected, while the French have engrossed the South Sea trade to themselves, and the Dutch encroach daily upon us, both in the East Indies and upon the coast of Africa. From hence it is that we have every year added to our burden, which was long ago greater than we could bear, whilst the Dutch have yearly lessened their proportions in every part of the war, even in that of Flanders, on the pretence of poverty.

"Whilst the Emperor has never employed twenty of his ninety thousand men against France, on account of the troubles in Hungary, which he would not accommodate, nor has suffered our vast expenses in Italy to be effectual on account of articles in which it did not suit with his conveniency to keep his word, and whilst each of the other confederates in his turn has, from some false pretence, or from some trifling consideration of private advantage, neglected to perform his part in the wars, or given a reason to the others for not performing theirs ; from hence it is that our fleet is diminished and rotten, that our funds are mortgaged for thirty-two and ninety-nine years, that our specie is exhausted, and that we have nothing in possession, and hardly anything in expectation, as a compensation to Britain for having borne the burden and heat of the day ; whilst Holland has obtained a secure and even formidable barrier ; . . . whilst the House of Austria has everything in hand, *à la Sicile près*, which they proposed by the war. . . . From hence, in one word, it is that our Government is in consumption, and that our vitals are consuming, and we must inevitably sink at once ; add to this, that if we were able to bear the same proportion of charge some years longer, yet, from the fatal consequences, should certainly miss the great general end of the war, the entire recovery of the Spanish monarchy from the House of Bourbon."

The means by which the Minister brought about the Peace have been almost universally condemned. His political correspondence has been generally regarded as " a mass of duplicity and falsehood." Mr. Lecky, while allowing that some separate explanations with the French was justifiable, condemns " the tortuous proceedings that terminated in the Peace of Utrecht" as " one of the most shameful pages in English history." Yet, allowing that many of the actions of the Ministers in conducting the negotiations appear indefensible, and that secret negotiations and arrangements behind the backs of allies are never pleasant to contemplate, there is something to be said for the course adopted. It must be remembered that peace without delay was absolutely necessary for the carrying out of the Tory policy. In 1706, in 1709, and in 1710, peace negotiations had been wrecked mainly through the obstinacy of the Dutch and Imperialists. Unless English Ministers entered into some understanding with the French, it was certain that the peace negotiations would again end in failure. The conduct of the Dutch and Imperialists throughout the war had been so selfish, they had so often acted disloyally to England, they had so frequently broken the engagements of the Grand Alliance to suit their own convenience, that, allowing that a policy of retaliation was unworthy of Great Britain, it is quite impossible to sympathize with their rage and disappointment on finding that England was determined to make peace.

Again, in the latter part of 1710 and early part of 1711, the Tory Ministry was in a precarious position. " They stood," said Swift, " like an isthmus between the extreme

Tories and the violent Whigs." Public opinion was in favour of the expulsion of the Bourbons from Spain, and till public opinion had been educated it would have been dangerous to reveal the character of the negotiations. This uncertainty as to the reception of the terms of peace by the nation undoubtedly was one of the principal reasons of the secret correspondence with France. The premature discovery of the negotiations in 1711 would have probably led to the ruin, if not to the impeachment of the Ministers. Again, Ministers were far more dependent upon the royal favour than they are at the present day. The personal influence of the Queen on the body of the nation was immense. The accession of Anne had been followed by Whig defeats at the polling-booths, and by large Tory majorities. Had Anne taken umbrage at the character of the peace proposals and dissolved Parliament, there is no doubt that the reverence felt for her would have resulted in the return of a large Whig majority bent on vengeance. Until they felt assured of concessions that would satisfy all classes in England, especially the commercial class, the Ministers naturally did not think it advisable to declare openly their intention of taking no further part in hostilities against the French. This, it seems, is the true explanation of the means adopted by Oxford and Bolingbroke to bring about peace.

The terms, too, have been criticized by writers who obviously have never realized that the conclusion of peace was a matter of life and death to the Ministers, and that the opposition offered by the Dutch and Imperialists to any but the most extravagant conditions rendered Bolingbroke's task unusually difficult. No one would now assert that the Dutch secured a " barrier " which at all compensated them for their long and successful struggle against France. It is impossible not to regret what has been called the desertion of the Catalans, and writers have one and all written as though Bolingbroke had deliberately given up the Catalans to the vengeance of Philip. Bolingbroke was fully aware of the claim of our faithful Catalan Allies on English consideration. Again and again he had during the negotiations exerted himself on their behalf. After his visit to Paris in August, 1711, Torcy wrote that, in accordance with St. John's representations, " Le roi dépêche un courrier à Madrid et conseille au roi d'Espagne d'accorder un pardon aux Catalans, et je ne doute pas qu'il ne suive un aussi bon avis." As late as February the 3rd, 1713, he wrote to Strafford to insist on the restoration of the Catalans to their ancient privileges. Unfortunately for his reputation, Bolingbroke did not make the restoration of the Catalans to their ancient privileges and their protection from Philip's hostility one of the express conditions of the Peace, but his language to Strafford leaves no doubt that he thought there would be no difficulty in securing to them their rights. But during the months immediately preceding the conclusion of peace Bolingbroke's hands were full. Ministers could not meet Parliament till the Peace had been signed. The death of Louis XIV. mig.t take place any day; Anne's health was most precarious. All sorts of delays occurred. The Peace was signed at last with the greatest haste, and Philip's promise was taken as sufficient security. But the Catalans opposed the Peace, refused to lay down their arms, and so played into the hands of the Spaniards. Philip considered himself absolved from his promise, and so the unfortunate necessity of hurrying on the Peace of Utrecht led Bolingbroke into the oversight which has cast the greatest blot on his statesmanship.

No fault can be found with the advantages gained for Great Britain. Bolingbroke fully realized the importance of the possession of Gibraltar, and in establishing English influence in the Mediterranean, and in securing an advantageous position in North America, he anticipated the policy of the elder Pitt and of Lord Beaconsfield.

In gaining considerable trade concessions, he showed a clear appreciation of the fact that England's interests were colonial and commercial, rather than European and political. That foreign statesmen did not think he neglected English interests may be gathered from the fact that when Torcy, in the summer of 1711, was first made acquainted with the British demands in favour of their commerce, he felt convinced that the granting of them would throw the whole trade of the world into British hands. From Spain Bolingbroke obtained trading advantages then regarded as considerable, in virtue of an arrangement known as *The Asiento* compact, in accordance with which England was to enjoy the privilege of supplying for thirty years some portion of the Spanish colonies in South America, as well as the Spanish West Indies, with negroes. The further important privilege of sending annually one ship, of 500 tons burden, to Spanish South America with merchandise, was also secured. In procuring for English traders an opening in South America, Bolingbroke was successfully carrying out a policy which Elizabeth and Cromwell had in vain attempted to inaugurate. Henceforward English interests increase in South America, English trading forces its way into the Spanish colonies, and Walpole, in 1739, finds himself much against his will compelled to recognize the demands of English merchants and to continue Bolingbroke's policy.

Bolingbroke's Commercial Treaty with France marks the first though premature attempt to establish a policy of Reciprocity and anticipated the Commercial Treaty made with France by the younger Pitt in 1786. He had formed great hopes of the advantages to be gained from such a treaty.

"I believe it will be of no use," he had written during the negotiations to the Duke of Shrewsbury, "to insinuate to Monsieur de Torcy that as, among other things, the factious people here intend, by their opposition to the settlement of any trade with France, to keep the two nations estranged from each other, to cultivate the prejudices which have been formerly raised, and which during two long wars have taken deep root, and also to prevent the wearing of them out, which would be the natural necessary consequence of an open advantageous trade ; so we on our part, and the Ministers of France on theirs, ought to counterwork their designs, and to finish what relates to commerce more in the character of statesmen than of merchants."

But Bolingbroke was not to be permitted to carry out his liberal commercial policy, and the Treaty of Commerce was violently opposed by the trading classes. After a prolonged debate, in which the celebrated 8th and 9th Fair Trade clauses were defended by Arthur Moore, their draftsman, the defection of Sir Thomas Hanmer to the Opposition decided the fate of the Commercial Treaty, and the Protection system was saved by nine votes.

Bolingbroke himself in later days by no means regarded the Treaty of Utrecht with unmixed satisfaction. On his retirement in 1735 to Chanteloup, in Touraine, he wrote to Lord Cornbury :—

"I shall not be surprised if you think that the Peace of Utrecht was not answerable to the success of the war, nor to the efforts made in it. I think so myself, and have always owned, even when it was making and made, that I thought so."

And, in his letter to Sir William Wyndham, he says,

"I am far from thinking the Treaties or the negotiations which led to them, exempt from fault."

In the same letter he points out some of the reasons why the Peace was not altogether satisfactory. In consequence of the policy of the Whigs, each of the Allies had been taught "to raise his demands to the most extravagant height"; they had been encouraged to this, first, "by the engagements which we had entered into with several of them, and secondly, by the manner in which we had treated with France in 1710." The conduct of the Whigs was throughout most unpatriotic. Though a small minority of the nation, the Whig Party was far superior in intelligence to the bulk of their opponents. The Whig leaders were none the less animated with a bitter spirit of faction. Obstruction in domestic matters is well known in the Parliamentary history of the latter half of the nineteenth century, but during the last four years of Anne's reign the Whigs did all in their power to hamper and obstruct Ministers, who were engaged in one of the most difficult and diplomatic tasks ever presented to English statesmen. Bolingbroke's own convincing indictment of the disgraceful party spirit shown by the Whigs has, I believe, never been weakened by any specious defence.

"If the means employed to bring about the peace were feeble, and in one respect contemptible, those employed to break the negotiations were strong and formidable. As soon as the first suspicion of a Treaty's being on foot crept abroad into the world, the whole alliance united with a powerful party in the nation to obstruct it. From that hour to the moment the Congress of Utrecht finished, no one measure possible to be taken was omitted to traverse every advance that was made in this work, to intimidate, to allure, to embarrass every person concerned in it. This was done without any regard either to decency or good policy, and from hence it followed that passion and humour mingled themselves on each side. A great part of what we did for the peace, and for what others did against it, can be accounted for on no other principle."

Then again, Bolingbroke had little help from his colleagues, while his own relations with Oxford rendered his difficult task still more difficult. Oxford, who has been styled "the Prince of wire-pulling and back-stair intrigue," but of whose political skill there is no question, had early in 1711 begun to regard Bolingbroke in the light of a possible rival. Though like Walpole an excellent party manager, Oxford, partly owing to bad health, partly through his failure to establish his ideal government, had decidedly deteriorated. He was at this time a vacillating, feeble politician, a miserable, inarticulate debater, a man wanting as a rule in decision of character, deficient in any fixed principles of conduct or policy, timid, fond of procrastination. Bolingbroke was a brilliant orator, clear-sighted, remarkable for his iron will and resolution, full of self-confidence, capable of conceiving and carrying out a statesmanlike policy. It is not surprising that men so differently constituted should have gradually become alienated. Several minor matters had tended to sow distrust between them. The attack on Oxford by Guiscard was probably meant for Bolingbroke, and the latter's friends had openly stated their conviction that Bolingbroke deserved the glory which Oxford had then gained. During Oxford's absence at that time from the House of Commons Bolingbroke, when the matter of the thirty-five millions unaccounted for by the Whigs was under discussion, had refused to allow his friend Bridges, Paymaster of the Forces under Godolphin, to be attacked. After his recovery, Oxford appeared very seldom in the House, and from this time the rivalry between him and Bolingbroke may be said to have begun.

"Mr. Harley," he writes to Orrery on May the 18th, 1711, "since his recovery, has not appeared in the Council, or at the Treasury at all, and very seldom in the House of Commons; we, who are reputed to be in his intimacy, have very few opportunities of seeing him, and none of talking freely with him. As he is the only true channel through which the Queen's pleasure is conveyed, so there is and must be a perfect stagnation till he is pleased to open himself and set the water flowing."

Bolingbroke's failure to secure the coveted earldom in 1712 still further alienated the two Ministers, and, as might be expected under these circumstances, Oxford, during the course of the negotiations, was rather a hindrance than a help. His influence with the Queen, however, rendered him indispensable to a Ministry in days when the Sovereign's influence was enormous. The position held by Oxford is well described by Bolingbroke in the following sentence:

"His concurrence was necessary to everything we did by his rank in the State; and yet this man seemed sometimes asleep and sometimes at play."

Bolingbroke was thus throughout the negotiations in a position in which no English statesman, while carrying through Treaties of such magnitude as those signed at

Utrecht, ever found himself. He never had the full confidence of either the extreme or of the moderate Tories.
"The ship is rotten," said Swift on March the 4th, 1711;
"The crew all against the Ministry." In December, 1711,
Nottingham, with a following of extreme Tories, had
deserted the Ministry and joined the Whigs. The Whigs
openly intrigued in London with foreign envoys against the
Government; the residences of Gallas and of Buys became
in turn the headquarters of the Whig Opposition; the lack
of decision among his colleagues hampered the course of the
negotiations, and Oxford, who was virtually Prime Minister,
regarded Bolingbroke with suspicion, envy, and resentment.

These considerations would incline an impartial reader to
view with some charitableness the means taken to bring
about the Peace of Utrecht, and to weigh well Bolingbroke's
own explanation of the deficiencies in that Treaty. The
wonder is that with so many impediments, and in the face
of so much hostility, with the possibility of the Queen's
death at any moment before him, Bolingbroke should have
during these two long years conducted the negotiations with
such energy and firmness, and, on the whole, with such
success. The Peace of Utrecht was a great peace, and not
unworthy of the statesman who negotiated it.

In the European struggles of the eighteenth century, the
union of France and Spain against England came about
not by dynastic but by commercial and colonial considerations. As long as there was any likelihood of Philip assert-
ing his claim to the French crown, there was hostility
between the two courts; but, as soon as Louis XV. had a
son, dynastic jealousies disappeared, and the countries found
a common ground of union in hostility to England's colonial
and commercial policy. That the Pyrenees ceased to exist
during a great part of the eighteenth century was not due
to the foreign policy of Bolingbroke in allowing a Bourbon
to rule in Spain, but to the inevitable trading rivalry

between England on the one hand, and France and Spain on the other.

The War of the Spanish Succession occupies a very important position in the second Hundred Years' War between England and France. For, though it was not till the Peace of Paris in 1763 that England could claim to be victor in the struggle, the power of France never recovered from the effects of the war which was ended by the Peace of Utrecht. France never could again, till the Revolution, adopt, with any chance of ultimate success, the aggressive attitude assumed by Louis XIV. She never recovered from the financial difficulties which the Spanish Succession War brought on her, and the army never regained its prestige till the events following 1789 gave her new life and energy. From 1713, too, her social difficulties became each year more serious.

To England the year 1713 is also a landmark, but not in the history of her decline. For the marvellous expansion that was in store for her, England required a long period of peace, and the Treaty of Utrecht, like the Peace of 1815, was followed by an extraordinary industrial development In breaking the power of France, and in enabling England to escape with advantage to herself from a costly war, and so to prepare for that immense colonial and territorial development which gave her Canada and eventually India, Bolingbroke played an important part.

It is well to remember that the Tory policy of interfering as little as possible on the Continent, of strengthening the navy, of attacking the colonial possessions of our enemies and sweeping the seas was the policy followed in very similar circumstances by both the elder and the younger Pitt. And to Bolingbroke must be given the credit of having in a most remarkable way attempted to carry out a foreign policy so successfully adopted in the Seven Years' War and in the struggle against Napoleon.

CHAPTER IV

THE SUCCESSION QUESTION.

1713-1714.

Possibility of a Stuart Restoration—Bolingbroke's real policy—Reasons
for the belief that he was a Jacobite—Opinion of Mr. Wyon—State
of politics on conclusion of Peace of Utrecht—The Jacobites, the
Hanoverian Tories, the Neutrals—Reconstruction of the Ministry—
The Crisis—Unpopularity of Harley's trimming policy—The Tories
rally round Bolingbroke—His extreme measures—Activity of the Whigs
—Attempt to bring the Electoral Prince into England—Rage of the
Queen—Reward offered for apprehension of the Pretender—End of the
Session, July 9—Approach of the Crisis—Dismissal of Oxford, July 27
—The Treasury to be put in Commission—Difficulty in choosing Com-
missioners—Illness of the Queen—Shrewsbury appointed Treasurer—
Death of Anne—Ruin of Bolingbroke's plans—His failure due to
various causes—Policy and position of Shrewsbury—A consideration
of Bolingbroke's policy at the end of Anne's reign—Vigour of Whigs.

THE Peace of Utrecht was a great step towards the consolidation of the Tory party, but it was hardly concluded
before the party was once more divided by the *pressing question of the Succession.*

The possibility of a Stuart Restoration on the death of
Anne has often been debated. It has been the general
opinion, till very recent years, that the whole object of
Bolingbroke's policy was a Stuart Restoration, that all his
measures were taken with that end in view, and that, had
the Queen lived a month or two longer, the overthrow of the
Act of Settlement would have been followed by the return of
the Pretender to St. James's.

The Scotch Jacobites and the French Ministers were convinced that Bolingbroke was in the interest of the Pretender, and numerous letters from the French emissaries, Gaultier and D'Iberville, to Torcy can be quoted in support of their opinion. This was also the Whig view of Bolingbroke's policy. As early as November, 1710, Swift had written sarcastically that " a Secretary of State cannot resign but the Pretender is at bottom; the Queen cannot dissolve a Parliament but it is a plot to dethrone herself and bring in the Pretender." Walpole always declared that the leaders of the Whigs were fully aware of the Jacobite designs of the Tory Ministers. Every motive of party interest combined to induce the Whigs to adopt the cry that the succession was in danger as long as the Tories were in power.

That this view of Bolingbroke's policy was unsound may be gathered from the fact that, after the accession of George I., the efforts of the whole Whig party were never able to substantiate the accusations they brought forward. And the reason of their failure to do so is obvious. The Restoration of the Stuarts was no part of the policy of Oxford and Bolingbroke. The Protestant Succession was never in danger. Bolingbroke himself had no religious scruples which would have deterred him from accepting James Edward, had the country declared in his favour. But the project of a Restoration so long as the Pretender remained a Roman Catholic was never a feasible one, and both Oxford and Bolingbroke knew it.

On December the 28th, 1713, Bolingbroke had told D'Iberville that the Pretender had no chance of success: "Tant qu'il sera Catholique, pas même en épousant une princesse Protestante"; and in February of the next year Gaultier, writing a letter at, he says, Oxford's dictation to the Pretender, says plainly : " Si vous voulez succéder surement à la reine votre sœur, il est absolument nécessaire que vous dissimuliez votre religion." Speaking of the accession of George I., Bolingbroke, in his *Letter to Sir William Wynd-*

ham, declares plainly that " nothing is more certain than this truth, that there was at that time no formed design in the party, whatever views some particular men might have against His Majesty's accession to the throne " ; and, in his *State of Parties at the Accession of George I.*, he makes the following weighty statement:

" There was no design on foot during the last four years of Queen Anne's reign to set aside the succession of the House of Hanover, and to place the crown on the head of the Pretender to it. . . . Neither could a design of that nature have been carried on so long, though it was not carried into execution without leaving some traces, which would have appeared when such strict inquisitions were made. . . . . But, laying aside all arguments of the probable kind, I deny the fact absolutely ; and I have the better title to expect credit, because it could not be true without my knowledge, or at least suspicion, of it : and because even they who believed in it—for all who asserted did not believe in it—had no proof to produce, nor have to this hour but vain surmises, nor any authority to rest upon but the clamour of party."

During Anne's reign national interests were completely subordinated to party interests. For party motives a war, just and necessary in its earlier stages, had been unduly prolonged. Mainly for party motives, though at the time they happened to coincide with the national interests, the Peace of Utrecht was made. Party motives led the Whigs to oppose by every means in their power the progress of the negotiations ; and the same motives, the same desire for place, prompted them to declare after the accession of George I. that all Tories were Jacobites. Swift, who was intimate with both Oxford and Bolingbroke, always declared his utter disbelief that the Act of Settlement was in any danger.

" Had there ever been," he writes in 1716, " the least overture or interest in bringing in the Pretender, during my acquaintance with the last Ministry, I think I must have been very stupid not to have picked up some discoveries or suspicions."

Lord Peterborough, too, on his deathbed declared that he knew Bolingbroke had no scheme for a Stuart Restoration.

To hastily conclude that the whole aim of the Tory Ministry, during Anne's later years, was to effect the return of James Edward is to misunderstand the position of both Oxford and Bolingbroke. The former, though ostensibly leader of the Tory party, was a Tory by accident. He had no real sympathy with High Church principles; he had little in common with the country gentlemen who were the rank and file of his followers. He was the head of a thorough-going Tory Government by no wish of his own, but by force of circumstances, which no one regretted more than himself. Like Marlborough, Shrewsbury, and Somerset, Oxford was an opportunist. He was not " insincere " in the sense in which Bolingbroke applied the term to him. He was certainly " unsound " in the matter of Toryism, as Bolingbroke conceived Toryism; but throughout Anne's reign he acted according to his lights, and to his theory of Government, with absolute consistency. Like Anne, he was always desirous to avoid throwing himself into the hands of a party. Like Bolingbroke, he had formed in his own mind a very distinct conception of a perfect form of government. According to Oxford, a Government should not be composed of violent politicians, like the members of the Whig junto, or of the October Club, men whose actions bore the impress of party bias. On the contrary, Ministers should be chosen from among moderate men, who would avoid the Scylla of extreme Whiggism and the Charybdis of violent Toryism. In this ideal Ministry moderate Tories should certainly preponderate, but the presence of a few of the more statesmanlike of the Whigs would act as a check on the partisan spirit of the extreme Tories. As soon, therefore, as any Government tended in his opinion to become a cabal of party politicians, Oxford, though himself a Minister, at once threw all his influence in the scale against his own colleagues. In 1704 he had intrigued successfully against Rochester and Nottingham; in 1707 he employed all his powers to upset Godolphin, and with him the Whig theory of Government by party; in 1710 he attempted to form a moderate and comprehensive Government; and in 1713 and 1714 he took up a position of passive opposition to the great body of his own followers, who viewed with dislike his schemes of compromise and moderation, and who had begun to look to Bolingbroke for guidance.

That statesman's ideal Government was very far removed from that designed by Oxford. He had no real sympathy with the High Church temper of many of the Tories, and with regard to the Succession question he was an opportunist. But he had a distinct programme and a clear political ideal. The consolidation of Toryism had nothing necessarily to do with Jacobitism, and was to be carried out, irrespective of all questions connected with the succession.

It is quite possible that had Bolingbroke only found sufficient time and opportunity; had he not been hampered by the Queen's hesitation to dismiss Oxford, and by his own want of influence over the whole of the Tory party before Anne's death, his scheme, though reactionary, might have been realized. A series of Acts would for a few years have protected the Church and country interest, and during those years the influence of the Church would have become so widely extended that there would have been no cause to fear that "any rich or factious body of men" would be in a position to choose "an ill majority of the House of Commons." Such was the opinion held by Swift, who advocated immediate and sweeping measures. And Bolingbroke, "playing the part of an orthodox Tory," had every intention of carrying out a definite and ably conceived policy.

His immediate object, then, was the establishment of a strong Tory Government to carry out a Tory policy in the interests of the Church and landed gentry, at home and abroad. He wished to succeed Oxford as First Minister, to place the whole administration in the hands of the Tories, and to make the Tory party master of the situation. He would then be able to dictate his own terms to either George or the Pretender. He had no intention of effecting a *coup d'état* after the manner of a Monk, or even of a Bonaparte. Bolingbroke was a statesman, and looked to realizing his scheme by means of constitutional forms.

Bolingbroke was never a Jacobite, that is to say, he never had any settled design of bringing in James Edward. That he had dealings with Jacobite agents and delivered himself of Jacobite sentiments is true. But it was necessary to gain over the Jacobite section in England, in order to secure a strong position at Anne's death. It was also politic, seeing how impossible it was to penetrate into the future. That he had intrigued with the Pretender is undoubted ; but who had not ? Godolphin, Marlborough, Oxford, Jersey, all were tarred with the same brush. Bolingbroke, like most of the politicians of the day, negotiated with both the Elector and the Pretender. The unmistakable preference of George for the Whigs tended undoubtedly to incline the Ministers to weigh seriously the chances of the Pretender ; but Bolingbroke's immediate object was, by consolidating the Tory party, to command the situation on the Queen's death. The Tory Government would then be ready for any contingency. If, contrary to expectation, the nation declared for James Edward, or if the Act of Settlement was upheld and George succeeded, the Tories would be strong enough to secure an arrangement favourable to their party.

But Bolingbroke was never anxious for an unconditional Restoration, at any rate until he had consolidated the Tory party. Had James Edward returned, like Charles II., free and unfettered, before the " scheme of four years' modelling " had been carried out, the Tory position would have been by no means an enviable one.

"The Tories," wrote Bolingbroke years later to Wyndham, "always looked on a restoration of the Stuarts as sure means to throw the whole power of Government into their hands. I am confident that they would have found themselves deceived."

When, however, all was uncertain; when the Queen might die any day, and the crisis be upon the Ministers; when Oxford, overcome by the uncertainty and difficulty of his position, had lost all power of action, the only man who showed the qualities of a statesman, who had any fixed policy, was Bolingbroke. During the fifteen months that elapsed between the conclusion of peace and the Queen's death, he made a determined effort to reconstruct Toryism on a sound basis. But events were against him. The dissensions among his supporters aided the vigorous attacks of his opponents, and just when it seemed that the principal obstacles in the way of success were removed, when a few weeks would probably have seen the Tory party in a strong position, the Queen died, and Bolingbroke's opportunities as a statesman were over.

The Peace of Utrecht had been hurried on, in order to clear the ground for the consolidation of the Tory party. "The Peace," he said, "had been judged with reason to be the only solid foundation whereupon we could erect a Tory system." But Bolingbroke's hopes were from the first doomed to disappointment. The conclusion of the Peace, so far from clearing the ground, and rendering his efforts to "erect a Tory system" which should defy all the vicissitudes common to political parties, brought with it grave difficulties. "Instead of gathering strength either as a Ministry or as a party, we grew weaker every day." Many of the terms of the Peace were unpopular even in England, and the Whigs seized the first opportunity of criticizing the Treaties of Peace and Commerce which were laid before Parliament in May. The Commercial Treaty which, if carried, would have established Free Trade with

France, was thrown out by a union of Whigs and Hanoverian Tories. " The very work," wrote Bolingbroke with reference to the Peace of Utrecht, " which ought to have been the basis of our strength, was in part demolished before our eyes, and we were stoned with the ruins of it." Early in 1714 the Whigs, supported by many Tories, and indeed by the general feeling of the country, criticized the absence of any satisfactory efforts on the part of the Ministers in favour of the unfortunate Catalans, and voted an address to the Queen, asking her to renew her efforts for the expulsion of the Pretender from Lorraine. It was with some difficulty that the Tories carried in both Houses a motion of approval of the Treaties of Peace. The Whigs had, however, raised the cry of " Danger to the Succession," and the Tory strongholds were shaken, while dissensions had already broken out among the supporters of the Government.

The Tory party was during these years clearly divided into three branches, the Jacobites, the Hanoverian Tories, and the Neutrals. Of these the most insignificant in point of numbers were the Jacobites—the party which firmly believed in hereditary right, and desired, under any circumstances, to bring about the Restoration of the Stuarts. Swift declared the party, exclusive of Papists and Nonjurors, did not number five hundred : " and, amongst these, not six of any quality or consequence." In their ranks must be numbered Ormonde, Mar, Buckinghamshire, and Atterbury. The Peace of Utrecht was no part of the Jacobite programme, for peace with France destroyed all hope of securing French aid—so essential for the realization of their schemes. But their relations with the Tory party compelled them to support the pacific policy of the Government.

The Hanoverian Tories, or Whimsicals, those " odd animals," as Lockhart calls them, were the men who were devotedly attached to the Church of England. In the

House of Lords this party, under Nottingham, had in December, 1710, voted with the Whigs against the Government, on consideration of securing the support of the Whigs in passing the Occasional Conformity Bill. "They were Churchmen first and legitimists afterwards." They represented the views held by the more enlightened and discriminating of the Tories, who were ready to uphold loyally the Act of Settlement if their ecclesiastical principles were not at stake. In the House of Commons their leader was Sir Thomas Hanmer, an ardent Hanoverian. It was the coalition of Hanmer and his party with the Whigs that wrecked Bolingbroke's Commercial Treaty with France. Bolingbroke had no patience with them. "As soon as the Treaties were perfected and laid before Parliament, the scheme of these gentlemen began to disclose itself entirely. Their love of the Peace, like other passions, cooled by enjoyment."

The revolt of these Hanoverian Tories shows that Bolingbroke had as yet by no means secured the confidence of a most influential section of his own party.

The Neutrals represented the great mass of the party. For the most part country gentlemen, their views on the Succession question were undecided; they hated Whigs, Nonconformists, and the moneyed interest. They dreaded Popery and French influence; at the same time they detested all Germans. They wished to see the interests of the country gentlemen and of the Church supreme in the Government. They desired a Tory king. Bolingbroke was their avowed leader, and Bolingbroke's Tory system would have suited them admirably. But Bolingbroke never secured the full confidence of either the country gentlemen or the country clergy. He never was a Churchman; he never understood his own followers, and he failed entirely to secure their hearty co operation. His reputation as a dissolute man of the world, talented, but none the less sceptical, caused him to forfeit in great measure their respect. This was undoubtedly serious, for the success of his efforts in 1713 and 1714 depended in great measure on the amount of support he could secure from the bulk of the Tory party.

The Government was evidently far from being strong or united. The successful attack of the Whigs, aided by the Tory secession on the Commercial Treaty, had shaken their position. Bolingbroke attributed the rejection of that Treaty to Oxford's bad management, and by July the feud between the two Ministers became most serious to the stability of the Government. The Queen's health was precarious; the Court of Hanover was known to be hostile to the Tories, and it was clear that the accession of the Elector would be followed by a series of merciless attacks on the Tory Ministers. There is no doubt that had Bolingbroke possessed sufficient influence with the Queen, and had not been hampered by Oxford, he would, in the summer of 1713, have strengthened his hold in the country by removing all Whigs from positions of authority, and giving their posts to supporters of his policy. Seeing the Tory party firmly established, the Elector would have had no choice but to enter into an arrangement which would, at any rate, have secured the Tories from the vengeance of the Whigs. Though unable to carry out his policy in its entirety, Bolingbroke, by dint of his determined will, did, however, bring about some important changes, calculated to place his party on a more stable basis. The interchange of letters between him and Oxford on July the 25th and the 27th was followed by the partial reconstruction of the Ministry. Dartmouth became Privy Seal, and Bromley, in November, succeeded Dartmouth as Secretary of State for the Southern Department. Wyndham was made Chancellor of the Exchequer in November, and a third Secretaryship was revived for Mar, who was to have charge of Scottish affairs. Ormonde had been secured by the

Wardenship of the Cinque Ports, and Atterbury and Robinson were made Bishops of Rochester and London respectively. The result of these changes was that a Secretary of State now sat in the House of Commons, and the correspondence with France was at last in Bolingbroke's own department. These changes, moreover, strengthened the position of the Ministry, and illustrates clearly the line that would have been taken by Bolingbroke had he only been at the head of affairs. He, and he alone, could have guided the Administration safely through the difficulties that beset it. In August, 1713, Parliament was dissolved, and Bolingbroke, whose relations with his wife were somewhat strained, spent the autumn at Ashdown Park with his dogs and horses. The country was still decidedly Tory, and Anne's last Parliament met with a strong Tory majority.

During the autumn Bolingbroke's influence at Court had continually increased. He had secured the friendship of Mrs. Masham ; he was in constant attendance on the Queen ; he exercised an extensive supervision over foreign affairs, the Irish administration, and the business of the Admiralty. His influence at Court was growing stronger each week, and we read how on December the 23rd he wrote eighteen letters in order that he might spend an undisturbed Christmas Day and the succeeding fortnig t with the Queen and Mrs. Masham. But on Christmas Eve Anne was taken ill, and for two weeks she was in a critical condition. All through January, 1713-14, alarming reports were in circulation, and the nation was in a state of feverish excitement. The stocks fell, and there was a panic in the Exchange. Prior, who was in Paris, was seized with alarm :—

"If," he said, "the prospect be dreadful to the masters of Mortimer Castle, Hinton St. George, Stanton Harcourt, and Bucklebury, what must it be to friend Matt ?"

Steele at once published his *Crisis*, which was immediately answered by Swift's *Public Spirit of the Whigs*. The Tory chiefs had again a splendid opportunity of carrying out Bolingbroke's scheme, of taking vigorous measures, and of securing to the Tories a monopoly of power. Anne had been for the moment roused to great anger at the conduct of the Whigs. Had the Ministers been united, they might have induced the Queen to lay aside her policy of moderation, and " act a clear game with the Tories." But Bolingbroke had not the supreme control of affairs, Oxford made no attempt to carry out a scheme with which he had no sympathy, the opportunity was lost, and Anne returned to her former policy of governing by compromise and conciliation. Even at this crisis it is plain that Bolingbroke had no definite schemes for a Jacobite Restoration, for on April the 13th, 1714, he wrote:—

" What will happen no man is able to foretell ; but this proposition is certain, that if the members of the Church of England lay aside their little piques and resentments, and cement closely together, they will be too powerful a body to be ill-treated."

It had become quite evident to him, at the beginning of 1714, that no more time must be lost, or the death of the Queen would find the Tories utterly disorganized. The strained relations and conflicting views of the Tory leaders were reflected in the jealousies and rivalries which had penetrated deep into the ranks of their supporters. At a time when order and decisive counsels were of the utmost importance there was only confusion and vacillation. " The party," wrote Bolingbroke (in April), " stands at gaze, expecting the Court will regulate them, and lead them on ; and the Court seems in a lethargy." And again at the same time he declared: " The prospect before us is dark and melancholy, and what will be the end, no man can foretell." His difficulties with the Treasurer became each day more serious. Oxford had hitherto insisted on continuing his favourite policy of compromise, of trying to conciliate the Whigs, of attempting to run with the hare and hunt with the hounds. Godolphin's Lord-Lieutenants were still supreme in the counties. The country remained to a great extent in Whig hands. In the *Lockhart Papers* we see the expression of a deep discontent.

"Several of the leading men of the October Club thought it now high time to push matters a little more briskly ; they had hitherto supported the Lord Oxford, and, now that Peace was concluded, they represented to him that they expected the performance of what was often promised, and what was absolutely necessary for the Queen's, his own, and their, security."

These men were not at all satisfied with Oxford's attempts to put them off with soft words, and they began to look to Bolingbroke, and :—

"thought that they had gained a great point if they could draw him in to set himself at their head ; and this he was ready enough to do, as, by his frank way of behaviour, he had already gained a great interest, affected daily to be more and more popular, and aimed at nothing less than being Prime Minister of State."

They accordingly interviewed Bolingbroke, who declared himself in entire agreement with them, and promised that he would carry out resolute and steady measures. They then decided to support him and to follow his directions, which were that they should act with caution and not "fly in the face of the Ministry, seeing it might probably prevent matters being brought about to their satisfaction." It was indeed absolutely necessary that the condition of affairs should be changed without delay. The whole Government of the country must be placed in the hands of the Tories, the leadership of the party must be wrested from the incapable hands of Oxford, and the administration completely reorganized. According to Bolingbroke, the Treasurer thought only of making himself safe in the future, and therefore tried to conciliate the Whigs, and adopted a temporizing policy which pleased no one. His only determined view was to raise his own family. He was "eternally agitated backwards and forwards." The ultimate end of his policy never extended farther than living from day to day." Being suspicious, he judged ill of all mankind, and was so credulous that, Bolingbroke asserts, "he never knew a man so capable of being the bubble of his own distrust and jealousy." Even as late as in the winter of 1713-14 he might have regained the confidence of the whole party if he had chosen, and Bolingbroke asserts: "he would have stifled his private animosity, and would have acted under him with as much zeal as ever." But Oxford lost his opportunity, and at the beginning of 1714 had no following; Bolingbroke had completely superseded him in the estimation of the Tory party. The old friendship between them was completely at an end. Bolingbroke's mind was made up; he determined to seize the leadership of the Tories. Measures were at once adopted to satisfy the Tory squires. Resolutions were passed in both Houses sanctioning the Peace; Steele was expelled the House of Commons for having written the *Crisis*. In order to placate the extremists of the Church of England a most tyrannical measure, called the Schism Act, was introduced in May, with the double object of pleasing the Tories and of placing the compromising Oxford in a dilemma. A violent quarrel ensued between the Ministers. Swift at length brought them together in Mrs. Masham's house, and used all his efforts to reconcile them. He saw, however, that the quarrel was beyond all chance of reconciliation, and in July Oxford voted against some articles inserted in a Commercial Treaty with Spain by Bolingbroke.

During this period of Tory activity, the Whigs had been far from idle. At the end of April, shortly after their success in carrying the resolution about the removal of the Pretender from Lorraine, the leaders held a meeting, at which it was settled that a member of the House of Hanover ought if possible to be resident in England at such a critical period. The rage of the Queen at this suggestion; her refusal to see Schutz who, prompted by the Whigs, had demanded the Electoral Prince's writ, as Duke of Cambridge; the issue of the writ; the letters of the Electress Dowager and of the Elector to Anne, asking for the removal of the Pretender from Lorraine, and intimating the desirability of the presence of the Electoral Prince in England, followed by Anne's letter of May the 30th, which hastened the end of the Electress Dowager, and by the mission of Clarendon to prevent the possibility of the Electoral Prince setting out for England—are all well-known episodes in the dramatic history of these six months. Just before the prorogation of Parliament two important events took place. The Whigs had brought forward a motion for paying the Hanoverian troops the arrears said to be due to them for their services during the campaign, when the English Army under Ormonde declined to aid the Allies. After a consultation in Bolingbroke's office, the Tories succeeded in getting this motion laid aside. The Whigs made a great outcry, and asserted that the Tory connection with the Pretender was now proved, the Tories maintaining that the Succession had nothing to do with the affair, but that, "if gentlemen were pleased to put that construction upon it, they were at liberty, for them." Lockhart, however, says distinctly, that the result of the debate encouraged the Jacobites, and that, if Bolingbroke had followed up the blow, there was nothing too difficult to be accomplished. He goes on to say that there was a general impression that the restoration of James would shortly take place, and declares that Bolingbroke assured those Jacobites with whom he was intimate that a little more patience was necessary till he had purged the Army, got rid of Oxford, and placed the Government in sure hands. But on June the 27th, without any warning, the Queen and Council issued a Proclamation, offering a reward of £5,000 for the capture of the Pretender. The Jacobites were furious, finding, as Lockhart quaintly puts it, that "their wine was suddenly mixed with water."

Bolingbroke had some difficulty in soothing his followers. He pretended that Oxford, with the help of Shrewsbury, was the author of the proclamation, in order to annoy him : he told Gaultier that he dared not oppose it, as Oxford's friends had for the last two months declared that his (Bolingbroke's) attempt to restore the Pretender was the real cause of the quarrel between them.

There is no doubt that Oxford wished at this time to discredit his colleague by fixing on him the stigma of Jacobitism. Baffled for the moment by Bolingbroke's assent to the issue of the Proclamation, Oxford then attempted without success to lessen his influence and damage his reputation by assisting in getting up a charge of bribery against Arthur Moore.

It is quite possible, too, that Bolingbroke hoped that the publication of the Proclamation, which Oxford expected, would quiet the alarmists, and would reveal to the Jacobites the extent of the Treasurer's insincerity. On July the 9th the session came to an end, the Queen in her Speech omitting all mention of the House of Hanover.

The open attacks of the Whigs and the insidious opposition of Oxford had all told on Bolingbroke during this trying session. Rarely has a statesman had to contend with such difficulties. " If my grooms did not live a happier life," he wrote to Swift, "than I have done this great while, I am sure they would quit my service."

Since the opening of the year, in spite of his quarrel with Oxford, the lethargy of the Court, and the indifference of many of his party, Bolingbroke had devoted all his energies to carrying out his policy. He had vigorously attacked his opponents, he had also made some progress in placing Tories in all important posts in the State. Tories had been promoted to colonelcies in the Army ; the Common Council of London had been placed in Tory hands. Time was all that Bolingbroke required for the complete triumph of his policy. During these months there was a general fear pervading the country that the succession was in danger. The Whigs acted throughout with vigour, the Tories with irresolution. A motion, " That the Protestant Succession was in danger under the present administration," was supported by the Hanoverian Tories. Bolingbroke had long seen the necessity of leaning on the Jacobite wing of his party in his attempt to make his position secure. The Schism Act had gained for him the full support of the Church ; by his nomination of Clarendon as envoy to Hanover, to prevent the Electoral Prince from coming to England, he had indicated his superiority to Oxford in the royal councils ; and Oxford had shown in June, by his offer of resignation—which was refused owing to the difficulty of appointing a successor— that he recognized the supremacy of Bolingbroke in the Tory party. It was evident that, before long, Oxford would no longer be an obstacle in the way of his brilliant colleague's policy.

Mrs. Masham was entirely in Bolingbroke's interest. Even the Duchess of Somerset, whose daughter had married Sir William Wyndham, ranged herself on the side of the opposition to the Treasurer. An inquiry into the negotiations with regard to the Treaty of Commerce with Spain was instituted early in July, in spite of the opposition of Bolingbroke. This proved damaging to the Government, and the prorogation of Parliament on July the 9th alone saved Bolingbroke from severe criticism.

On July the 27th, Oxford was dismissed from his office. Anne's reasons were that he was " seldom to be understood, was untrustworthy, unpunctual, ill-mannered, and disrespectful." The same day Bolingbroke entertained at dinner, at his house in Golden Square, the principal members of the Opposition—Stanhope, Pulteney, Craggs, and Walpole ; and Walpole himself admitted that this was done for the purpose of arranging the terms of a Coalition. The negotiations broke down on Bolingbroke's refusal to insist on the removal of the Pretender " to such a distance as would prevent his interference in the affairs of England." Bolingbroke, who had assured the Whigs of his good wishes to the Protestant Succession, gave as a reason for his refusal his inability to procure the Queen's consent to such a measure.

It is a great pity so little is known of the proceedings at this memorable dinner. Erasmus Lewis wrote to Swift on July the 29th to tell him that " Mercurialis entertained Stanhope, Craggs, Pulteney, and Walpole. What if the Dragon (Harley) had done so ?"

It was after this failure to effect a Coalition that Bolingbroke seems to have felt that he could only rely on the extreme members of his party whom he had gained over— and this is the view of von Ranke—by simulating strong Jacobite proclivities. But he had little time to inaugurate any policy ; he was not appointed to succeed Harley, though he remained, till the Queen's death, practically Prime Minister, and during his short tenure of power sent Swift £1,000 from the Exchequer. It is difficult to assign reasons for passing him over. Shrewsbury, who was regarded with great favour by Anne, and who was never a Tory, may have opposed his appointment. Probably the dislike with which Anne always regarded Bolingbroke, coupled with "that fatal irresolution inherent in the Stuart race," prevented her from placing at the head of affairs the ablest man of the day. It must also be remembered that Anne was as strongly opposed as Oxford to a partisan Government, and that she never showed any sympathy with Bolingbroke's scheme for a united Tory administration. The Treasury was to be put in Commission, with Sir William Wyndham at the head of it ; but the difficulty in choosing the other names was so great, that the Cabinet sat up till 2 a.m. on July the 28th, without being able to choose four Tories capable of undertaking the office. It was arranged that the Council should meet at

Kensington on the 29th, but the violent altercations raging round her had shaken Anne's health. "She could not out-live it," she said, and the morning of the 29th found her too ill to do any business, and the meeting of the Council was postponed. Early on Friday the 30th she was seized, prob-ably with apoplexy, and was insensible for two hours. The members of the Cabinet, who were in constant consultation at the Cockpit, on hearing the alarming news, hurried at once to Kensington, where the Queen lay manifestly dying. In the Council-chamber they received the report of the physicians, which was most unfavourable. It was deter-mined to abandon the idea of putting the Treasury in Com-mission, and Bolingbroke proposed that Shrewsbury should act as Treasurer. The physicians having reported that the Queen might be spoken to, Bolingbroke, about 1 o'clock in the afternoon, told her of the recommendation of the Council, and Anne placed the Treasurer's staff in Shrewsbury's hand. Those two advocates of compromise, Somerset and Argyll, who were still Privy Councillors, arrived at Kensington the same day, and were reinforced by many leading Whigs. The Privy Council sat all that day and the ensuing night. Measures were at once taken to secure the safety of Portsmouth and the tranquillity of London, and it became evident that Shrewsbury's influence was entirely at the disposal of the Whigs, and would be used to carry out the Whig programme.

At 7 o'clock on the morning of Sunday, August the 1st, Anne died.

Bolingbroke asserted a few days later that " his measures had been so well taken, that in six weeks matters would have been placed in such a condition that he would have had nothing to fear." He had determined to fill all the posts in the new Government with staunch Tories, whether Jacobite, or not. Bromley, Mar, Atterbury, Harcourt, Or-monde, Buckinghamshire, and Wyndham were to have been the leading Ministers. And there is little doubt that, had he carried out the above scheme, such changes would have been effected in the country, that George would have been unable to carry on the Government except by means of a Tory Ministry.

During the interval which elapsed between Oxford's dismissal and Anne's death, Bolingbroke evidently had little power. It is probable, however, that, had the Queen lived for a few weeks longer, his well-known abilities would soon have secured him the adhesion of the whole Tory party. At the same time, Bolingbroke's statement made later in his letter to Wyndham, that "at the time of the Queen's death there was no 'formed plan' among the Tories for the restoration of the Stuarts," is quite correct. As it turned out, Anne's delay in dismissing Oxford had ruined Bolingbroke's chance of success. He himself says, when writing of Anne's unfortunate mistake in keeping Oxford in power :—

"We saw our danger, and many of us saw the true means of avoiding it ; but, while the magic wand was in the same hands, this knowledge served only to increase our uneasiness, and, whether we would or no, we were forced with our eyes open to walk on towards the precipice."

Then, Anne's dislike to the absolute supremacy of one party, combined with the dissensions within the Ministry over the appointment of Commissioners of the Treasury, kept matters in suspense, when decision was of vital importance.

Shrewsbury had been Bolingbroke's last hope. If he had declared unmistakably for the Tories, all might yet have been well. That enigmatical statesman was, however, destined to finally overthrow all Bolingbroke's schemes. He had never, indeed, been a Tory like Argyll and Somerset; he was equally opposed to the Whig junto and the October Club; he was in favour of mixed governments, and of a policy of conciliation : consequently he had no sympathy with Bolingbroke's system of "Thorough." He had aided in the events of 1688, and his influence largely contributed to the fall of the Whigs in 1710. Though vain and fickle, he enjoyed among Englishmen of his day the character of disinterestedness. He had till lately acted on behalf of the Government in France and in Ireland. In 1714 he had returned to London, and sided with Harley and the moderate Tories, rather than with Bolingbroke and the extremists. He had opposed several of the latter's violent measures, but had also at times supported him. He had, too, it appears, secured the Queen's confidence. Bolingbroke could not satisfy himself as to the real intentions of Shrewsbury. "How I stand with that man (Oxford) I know," he said a few days before the crisis, " but as to the other (Shrewsbury) I cannot tell." But when Anne lay dying, Bolingbroke, distracted by the divisions within the ranks of his own party, had no means of judging how far his own power of controlling events extended, and naturally turned towards the powerful and influential Shrewsbury, whom he had reason to believe would now support him. But the instinct of the King-maker was strong in Shrewsbury. For a second time he was destined to aid in overthrowing the hopes of the Stuarts. He had made up his mind that the Hanoverian cause was the winning one, and at once decided to make the position of the dynasty secure. He had his reward. When the list of the Regents was published after Anne's death, Shrewsbury's name alone of the Queen's last Ministry appeared. The vigour of Shrewsbury, Argyll, and Somerset—the middle party—backed by the strenuous support of the Whig chiefs, left no doubt that the Act of Settlement would be carried out, and that George would ascend the throne, which he believed he owed to the exertions of the Whigs on his behalf. " The Earl of Oxford was removed on Tuesday, the Queen died on Sunday," wrote Bolingbroke to Swift. " What a world this is, and how does Fortune banter us !"

CHAPTER V

BOLINGBROKE IN EXILE.

1714–1725.

Failure of the Schemes of Oxford and Bolingbroke—Accession of George I.
—Attitude of the Council of Regency towards Bolingbroke—His removal
from his Secretaryship—Seizure of the papers of Strafford and Prior—
Hostile attitude of Ministers—Alarm of Bolingbroke—His flight a fatal
mistake—His attainder—He enters the service of the Pretender—He
acts loyally in the Jacobite cause—His amusing description of James'
Council—James' character—Arrival of Ormonde in Paris—Death of
Louis XIV.—Failure of Jacobite rising of 1715—Causes of the failure—
Bolingbroke's dismissal from James' service—Berwick's testimony to his
ability—Bolingbroke attempts to secure the reversal of his attainder—
His Letter to Wyndham—His second marriage—Life at La Source—
Letters to M. de Pouilly—Voltaire's visit to La Source—His Pardon
passes the Great Seal, 1723—Bolingbroke visits England—Fails to conciliate Walpole—Aids Townshend and Walpole in their diplomatic
struggle against Carteret—Renewed endeavours to secure reversal of
his attainder—Their success, 1725—His return to England.

THE last days of the reign of Queen Anne proved fatal to
the realization of the schemes of both Oxford and Bolingbroke. The former had almost to the day of his loss of
office pursued his trimming policy, and had intrigued
against his colleagues just as he had formerly intrigued
against Godolphin and Marlborough. But his efforts to
check the advance of our modern system of Government by
party were all in vain. The whole tendency of the time
was against the existence of mixed Ministries. His ideas
on Cabinet Government proved, like Sir William Temple's
scheme for the reorganization of the Privy Council, incapable of being carried into effect. The bulk of the Whig
and Tory parties looked for strong united Ministries, and

were in no humour to listen to arguments in favour of Government with a divided Council, even though those arguments were urged by such distinguished politicians as Oxford, Somerset, and Shrewsbury.

Bolingbroke's great scheme, too, faded into thin air. That scheme holds a unique position in English Parliamentary history. Never before nor since has a responsible statesman endeavoured to put into execution so suddenly a plan which would have ensured the continuance of one party in power for an indefinite period. What Bolingbroke attempted to do openly in the interest of the Tories, Walpole in great measure effected by more insidious methods in the interest of the Whigs. But, while the latter only accomplished his object after some twenty years of steady labour, the former struggled to carry out his well-conceived plan within the short space of four years. To place the "Tory system" on a firm foundation, and to render it superior to all the vicissitudes of Parliamentary life, and proof against all the attacks from political opponents, had been the aim of Bolingbroke since 1710. When we consider that the realization of his scheme meant the continued exclusion of the Whig statesmen from power, the disfranchisement of the Nonconformists, as well as their exclusion from all share in the municipal and educational life of the country, and the continuance of the Church party and the landed gentry in the enjoyment, not only of political power, but also of all the privileges they had possessed before the Revolution of 1688—we cannot but wonder that this policy, so bold, so clearly defined, and so deliberately conceived, has not attracted more attention. The oft-repeated assertion, that all Bolingbroke's efforts were directed to the Restoration of the Stuarts, is as false historically as it is unfair to the memory of Bolingbroke himself. Towards the attainment of the great end he had in view, the firm establishment of Toryism, all his energies had been directed. That in carrying out a policy of such magnitude, including as it did the settlement of Europe after a long war, Bolingbroke had to employ methods which would at the present day be reprobated, is doubtless true. He himself, in a well-known and striking passage, has endeavoured to justify the tortuous ways which he had followed during his Secretaryship :—

"The ocean which environs us is an emblem of our Government ; and the pilot and the minister are in similar circumstances. It seldom happens that either of them can steer a direct course, and they both arrive at their port by means which frequently seem to carry them rom it ; but, as the work advances, the conduct of him who leads it on with real abilities clears up, the appearing inconsistencies are reconciled, and, when it is once consummated, the whole shows itself so uniform, so plain, and so natural, that every dabbler in politics will be apt to think he could have done the same." (*Bolingbroke's Works*, vol. i., pp. 23, 24).

In spite of the numerous obstacles and difficulties which would have daunted most men, Bolingbroke kept the end of his policy clearly in view. This policy was far from being one of sheer opportunism, dictated by the desire of mere power. That it was one of exclusion and proscription is obvious ; that it aimed at " securing those who had been principal actors in the Administration against future events," and at establishing the Tory party so firmly in power as to defy all accidents, is also true. But before criticizing too harshly a policy, which with all its defects speaks volumes for the statesman who conceived and wellnigh carried it out, it is only fair to compare it with the shilly-shallying attitude of Oxford, and to remember that Walpole's policy was in a great measure the same policy in the interest of the Whigs—having, moreover, on literature and religion a blighting and deadening effect, which we think would not have resulted from the policy of the Tory statesman.

The death of Anne ruined Bolingbroke's career as a Tory statesman. He was now barely thirty-six years old, and had already established a reputation which few men have ever enjoyed. His Parliamentary life began in 1701 ; it ended in 1714. During those thirteen years he had won for himself a foremost position in the great Tory party, had proved himself the ablest exponent living of Tory policy, had grappled successfully with most complicated Treaty negotiations, and, but for an accident, would undoubtedly have continued to guide the destinies of England. This position had been gained partly by reason of those immense powers of application which so astonished Swift, partly by his intellectual superiority to the bulk of the Tory party, partly by his marvellous eloquence. His speeches, none of which have come down to us, were looked back to in the days of Burke " as more priceless than the lost fragments of antiquity."

On Anne's death Atterbury had proposed to proclaim James III. at Charing Cross. But the activity of the Whigs in securing on the side of order all the resources of the Government, had destroyed all hope of a successful rising in favour of the Pretender. As Bolingbroke wrote to Strafford, " There never was yet so quiet a transition from one Government to another." Bolingbroke himself made a bold attempt to preserve his place in the new Government. It was quite uncertain how far George would consider his true interest to lie in conciliating the Tories, who formed a large majority of the nation. Bolingbroke, therefore, wrote a letter to the Elector, promising to serve him with honour and fidelity. Till an answer was received, he had to submit to the authority of the Council of Regency, which had been nominated by George. This council was mainly composed of leading Whig nobles, and of High Churchmen like Nottingham and Anglesea, who had in the past opposed the policy of Oxford and Bolingbroke. Of the late Ministers, Shrewsbury alone was found nominated one of the Regents. "The Council of Regency," wrote Bolingbroke to Sir William Wyndham, " which began to sit as soon as the Queen died, acted like a council of the Holy Office." They treated Bolingbroke with the greatest disrespect. " I received no mercy from the Whigs, and I deserved none," was his confession later. At the end of August George answered his letter by dismissing him from his Secretaryship, and appointing Townshend in his place. Though orders were sent to seize and seal up his papers, his Undersecretary, Thomas Hare, secured the most valuable, which were edited by Gilbert Parke in 1798. The arrival of George, on September the 18th, decided the fate of the Tories. The new King treated the late Ministers with studied insult. He attached himself unreservedly to the Whig party. And that party was determined to use the cry of " Danger to the Succession," in order to justify their vengeance on the Tories.

" The art of the Whigs," wrote Bolingbroke afterwards, " was to blend, as undistinguishably as they could, all their party interests with those of the Succession ; and they made the same factious use of the supposed danger of it, as the Tories had endeavoured to make, some time before, of the supposed danger of the Church."

Instead of holding a neutral position above all parties, George allowed the Whigs to make him a party King, the leader of a small, well-organized, and vindictive faction. The immediate result of the conduct of the Whigs was that the general disposition to Jacobitism increased daily among all ranks ; the ultimate result was that the great Tory party became by the arts of their opponents associated with Jacobitism, and remained powerless in Parliament till the accession of George III. At the new elections a large Whig majority was returned. Parliament met on March the 17th, 1715, and Bolingbroke, who had lived at Bucklersbury since his dismissal, led the Opposition in the House of Lords. There, in the debate on the address, Bolingbroke made his last speech in Parliament, in opposition to the insertion of a clause which implied that he and Oxford were traitors to the Protestant cause, and had injured England's welfare by the Peace of Utrecht. In the House of Commons Walpole openly declared that the Whig Ministers intended to punish the members of the late Government. The arrival of Prior in London on March the 25th, his friendly reception by Townshend, followed by his examination by a Committee of the Privy Council, decided Bolingbroke to fly. On the evening of March the 25th Bolingbroke was at Drury Lane, where he bespoke a play for the next night. The same evening he left London in disguise, travelled to Dover, where he wrote the letter to Lord Lansdowne, and on March the 28th crossed over to Calais. It is said that, on his way to Paris, he met Peterborough, who, still furious with him for concluding the Peace of Utrecht, passed him without a word.

Historians will always be divided on the subject of Bolingbroke's intentions at the time of Anne's death. Some writers do not hesitate to declare that his Jacobitism was undoubted, that he was intriguing for a Stuart restoration, and that it was only the want of sufficient time to enable him to perfect his preparations that prevented a declaration on behalf of James Edward on the day of Anne's death.

On July the 27th Anne had taken away the white staff of the Treasurer from Oxford, but though the Treasury was placed in commission, Bolingbroke, it is said, by putting suspected Jacobites into the vacant offices, was evincing a determination to place the Pretender on the English throne. Ormonde, of undoubted Jacobite tendencies, was certainly Warden of the Cinque Ports, but Bromley, Secretary of State in 1713, though a High Churchman, owed his position to Oxford; and Wyndham, the Chancellor of the Exchequer, and a close friend of Bolingbroke, was by no means an avowed Jacobite. It must be remembered, too, that Bolingbroke was far from being a *persona grata* with the Tory party, for the members of that party, as in 1688, were Churchmen before everything, and were not prepared to take action on behalf of the Pretender until he had definitely abjured his Roman Catholicism. D'Iberville had written to Torcy as late as May the 19th, 1714, that unless James Edward abjured his faith he would not receive the support of Bolingbroke.

After the accession of George I. the Jacobites in France undoubtedly expected to gain over Bolingbroke to their cause. On January the 6th, 1715, the Duke of Berwick stated in a letter to the Pretender that it was hoped that Bolingbroke would work for the cause of James III. by securing the support of several of the leading Tories. In a subsequent letter Berwick declares that Hanmer is too self-seeking to be of much use to the Jacobite cause, but that Bolingbroke " is the man I wish would work heartily." It is evident from these two letters, written in January, 1715, that *Bolingbroke was not yet regarded as an avowed Jacobite.* In fact, till the beginning of 1715 Bolingbroke appears to have hoped that George I. might employ him, and he seems to have satisfied himself that at any rate he was in no danger of any attack. But the Government of the " Venetian oligarchs" was determined to unravel all the negotiations preceding the Peace of Utrecht. Lord Strafford, who had been at Utrecht, was forced to surrender all his papers early in January, 1715, while at the same time the Earl of Stair, the English envoy in Paris, took possession of Prior's correspondence, which included Bolingbroke's private dispatches. It was quite evident that Bolingbroke's enemies intended to leave no stone unturned in order to secure his impeachment. " Had there been the least reason to hope for a fair and open trial," he wrote from Dover, when on his way to France, to Lord Lansdowne, " after having been already prejudiced unheard by two Houses of Parliament, I should not have declined the strict examination. I challenge the most inveterate of my enemies to produce any instance of criminal correspondence or the least corruption on any part of the Administration in which I was concerned."

Bolingbroke seems to have decided on flight in a moment of panic. He had just heard that Prior, then in the custody of a messenger, had been invited by Townshend to dinner. But there was nothing treasonable in Prior's correspondence. In his letter to Lansdowne, which was published, Bolingbroke says:

" I had certain and repeated information from some who are in the secret of affairs, that a resolution was taken by those who have the power to execute it to pursue me to the scaffold. My blood was to be the cement of a new alliance."

Marlborough had supplied him with the information; but in his *Letter to Sir William Wyndham*, Bolingbroke denies that he was moved by Marlborough's artifices. He afterwards declared that he left England upon mature reflection, not wishing to owe his security to the Whimsical Tories, and resolved not to consult with Oxford—whom he abhorred —about their mutual defence, or to suffer with him. He could not have made a worse blunder. Oxford stood his ground, was impeached, remained without trial in the Tower for two years, and then was publicly acquitted. Bolingbroke's flight was naturally construed to imply guilt. All it really implied was a want of moral fortitude, often the characteristic of impatient, mercurial natures like his, and quite compatible with the possession of a considerable amount of political courage. The report of Walpole's Committee of Secrecy, which was appointed, on Bolingbroke's flight, to examine all documents relating to the negotiations about the Peace, conclusively proves that, had Bolingbroke remained in England, his enemies could not have charged him successfully with high treason. But his flight had ruined his career, and left him at the mercy of his enemies. In September he was attainted of high treason, his property was confiscated, and he was condemned to death. His name was about the same time ordered to be struck from the roll of Peers.

Henceforward Bolingbroke was unable to re-enter Parliamentary life. He was later, it is true, permitted to return to England, where he became the organizer of a powerful opposition to Walpole. Like Pulteney, Shelburne, and Charles James Fox, the greater part of his life was spent in opposition. Politics, however, were far from being his only resource. His exile marks the beginning of a new period in his career, in which he combined a profound interest in politics with a devotion to literature and to philosophical and religious inquiry.

Till early in May he remained in Paris, where he was well known, and treated as a distinguished guest. He assured Stair, with whom he had a friendly interview, that while he remained in Paris he would have no dealings with the Pretender. In fact, he was very careful to avoid all entanglements with the Jacobites, who were in considerable numbers in the French capital. Caution, in fact, regulated all his actions while in Paris, for it was for some little time uncertain whether the Whig Government would push matters *à l'outrance*. On May the 10th he left Paris and proceeded to St. Clair, near Vienne, and towards the end of June he settled at Bellevue, near Lyons. Meanwhile his enemies in England had not been idle. Early in April a Committee of Secrecy had been formed to inquire into all the circumstances connected with the Treaty of Utrecht, and its report was presented to the House of Commons by Walpole on June the 9th. No delay took place in prosecuting the absent statesman, for the following day Walpole "formally impeached Bolingbroke of high treason." The charges against him were partly definite, partly indefinite. It was stated that he had betrayed England's allies, that he had sacrificed to France "the interests and honour" of the country, and that he had corresponded with the Pretender. In the middle of August a Bill of Attainder against Bolingbroke was brought in and carried in Parliament. Oxford, Ormonde, and Strafford were also at the same time impeached with Bolingbroke. The impeachment of Strafford for high treason was not proceeded with, and in July, 1717, Oxford, after two years' confinement in the Tower, was acquitted of all charges by the House of Lords. Ormonde, whose impeachment was voted on June the 17th, was very popular in London and in the country. Though no active steps were at once taken against him, he realized a few weeks later that his arrest was imminent, and on the night of July the 20th he fled to France, his flight implying that all rumours of a popular insurrection in England on behalf of the Pretender were unreliable.

Meanwhile Bolingbroke, before the Act of Attainder had been passed, had thrown in his lot with the Pretender. At the beginning of July, he received letters from Wyndham and from the Pretender himself. The former described the situation in England, where the clergy and populace were united in opposition to the Government. Riots were taking place not only in London, but also all over the Midlands; the popularity of Ormonde and Oxford was undoubted, Jacobite mobs had destroyed Dissenting meeting-houses, in Edinburgh the Pretender's health was openly drunk, the new King was unable to ingratiate himself with the mass of his new subjects. Wyndham apparently hoped for a revolution to take place shortly, for he urged Bolingbroke not to remain *neuter* when affairs were in "so critical, so unexpected, and so promising a situation." The letter from the Pretender invited Bolingbroke to hasten to confer with him at Commercy in Lorraine, and there, early in July, the interview, a momentous fact in the statesman's life, took place.

At Commercy he decided to join the Pretender, and this step, which has been styled "the rashest and the most regrettable " that he ever took, was no doubt the result of the reports which he had received of the unrest in England and Scotland.

But James Edward Stuart was a very different man from his predecessors. He was superstitious, timid, vacillating, and irresolute. He surrounded himself with Jesuit intriguers and numerous English, Scottish, and Irish adventurers. That he had any party ready to act was due, according to Bolingbroke, to the measures of the Whigs. "*Those measures*," he wrote, "*alone produced the troubles that followed, and dyed the royal ermines of a prince, no way sanguinary, in blood. I am far from excusing one party, for suffering another to drive them into rebellion; I wish I could forget it myself.*" He then points out "*that the very manner in which the rebellion was begun, shews abundantly that it was a start of passion, a sudden phrenzy of men transported by their resentment.*"

The history of the previous relations of the Tory Ministers with James might have led him to know what to expect. In 1714 Bolingbroke had complained to D'Iberville that James was surrounded by untrustworthy persons; that everything he says or does was known; that the name of every one he sees or corresponds with was instantly communicated to the Whigs. James had never taken any good advice. He had been strongly urged to communicate with England by means of Torcy alone, to leave Lorraine before the meeting of Parliament in 1714, to go perhaps to Venice where he could see his English partisans without suspicion, to give up his religion, or at least to simulate conversion. To his infinite credit, he declared in March, 1714, in very explicit and straightforward language, that under no circumstances would he surrender his religious beliefs, or pretend to change his religion for the sake of a crown. In other respects his actions were not so praiseworthy. He refused to leave Lorraine, and persisted in corresponding with his Scotch, and, what was worse, with his Irish partisans, men who, no matter how zealous in his cause, had no idea of the meaning of the words judgment and discretion. Bolingbroke's new relations with the Jacobites served only to bring out in stronger relief the flaws in James' own character, and the weak points in the Jacobite organization. The faithful Middleton, who had gone into exile with James II., and whose talents were considerable, had been practically driven from the Chevalier's service in December, 1713.

Bolingbroke was to find that the same influences which had proved too powerful for Middleton would bring about his own dismissal. In his *Letter to Sir William Wyndham* he gives a full account of his motives in joining James, and a most amusing description of James' frame of mind, and of the condition of the Jacobite party in Paris. It is impossible to accept the reason he gives in that letter for joining James. Resentment at the Bill of Attainder drove him, he declares, into the Jacobite ranks. The Bill of Attainder was not passed till September. He had adopted the Jacobite cause in July. In his first interview, the Chevalier talked to Bolingbroke " like a man who expected every moment to set out for England or Scotland, but who did not very well know for which." The truth was, his Scottish partisans were urging James to hasten his departure, without considering the advisability of waiting till the English Jacobites were prepared to rise. Berwick, an able soldier, had nominally the principal direction of James' affairs in France, but he had little power to influence James' decisions.

In his first interview with Bolingbroke at Commercy, the Pretender was probably justified from the accounts which had reached him in expecting " every moment to set out for England or Scotland." The rising of 1715 shows that both men had not underestimated the repugnance to the accession of George I. felt in the latter country. But while James urged an immediate Scottish expedition, Bolingbroke opposed any such precipitate action until simultaneous risings in England and Scotland, supported by French troops, arms, and money, could be organized. The presence of the Chevalier in Scotland when his flag was unfurled was also insisted upon. Having convinced James of the necessity of taking no precipitate action and of watching events in England, Bolingbroke departed for Paris on July the 23rd. There he was introduced to his Jacobite coadjutors.

"I found a multitude of people at work, and every one doing what seemed good in his own eyes ; no subordination, no order, no concert. . . . The Jacobites had wrought one another up to look on the success of the present designs as infallible. Care and hope sat on every busy Irish face. Those who could write and read had letters to show, and those who had not arrived at this pitch of erudition had their secrets to whisper. . . . Into such company was I fallen, for my sins."

There Bolingbroke continued to insist that all action should be postponed till a "formed plan" had been concerted and an organized scheme prepared. Had James given Bolingbroke full power, had he trusted him implicitly, had he followed his and Berwick's advice, the Jacobite movement in Scotland might have had results very serious to the stability of George's throne. But unfortunately James did not place full confidence in either Bolingbroke or Berwick, his two ablest advisers.

Bolingbroke's delineation of the character of James gives one a very clear explanation of the reasons of the failure of the rising of 1715 :—

"His religion is not founded on the love of virtue and the detestation of vice. . . . The spring of his whole conduct is fear—fear of the horns of the devil and of the flames of hell. . . . He has all the superstition of a Capuchin ; but I found in him no tincture of the religion of a prince. . . . I have heard the same description of his character made by those who knew him best ; and I conversed with very few among the Roman Catholics themselves who did not think him too much a Papist." Then he was far too sanguine. "He had been suffered to think that the party in England wanted him as much as he wanted them. There was no room to hope for much compliance on the head of religion when he was in these sentiments, and when he thought the Tories too much advanced to have it in their power to retreat ; and little dependence was at any time to be placed on the promises of a man capable of thinking his damnation attached to the observance, and his salvation to the breach, of these very promises."

It would hardly be expected that so sanguine a Prince would be willing to listen to the calm counsels of experienced men. Berwick had been in Spain during those important first seven months of 1714. He was strongly opposed to the expedition of 1715, unless careful arrangements were made for a rising in England. Actuated by a mean jealousy of the great French marshal, James deliberately chose the vain Ormonde as his adviser : a most fatal mistake, for he thus deprived himself of the help of the two men who alone could have assured him any reasonable chance of success. Ormonde's flight from England had ruined all chance of organizing a rising in England. He was a man of very different calibre to his grandfather, the staunch cavalier of the reigns of Charles I. and II. His flight and the death of Louis XIV. rendered, in Bolingbroke's opinion, the Pretender's expedition hopeless before it started.

" Two events," wrote Bolingbroke later to Wyndham, "soon happened, one of which cast a damp on all we were doing, and the other rendered vain and fruitless all we had done. The first was the arrival of the Duke of Ormonde in France, the other was the death of the King."

Ormonde had up to this time (August) been living in great style at Richmond, assuring the Jacobites abroad that he would remain in England ready to act. In order to get French aid, Bolingbroke had declared to the French Ministers that Ormonde's appearance in the West of England would be the signal for 20,000 men to rise.

" We had sounded the Duke's name high. His reputation and the opinion of his power were great. The French began to believe that he was able to form and lead a party, that the troops would join him, that the nation would follow the signal whenever he drew the sword. . . . But when in the midst of all these bright ideas they saw him arrive almost literally alone, when to excuse his coming I was obliged to tell them that he could not stay, they sunk at once from their hopes ; and that which generally happens happened in this case, because they had had too good an opinion of the cause, they began to form too bad a one. Before this time, if they had no friendship for the Tories, they had at least some consideration and esteem. After this I saw nothing but compassion in the best of them, and contempt in the others."

The flight of Ormonde was followed shortly afterwards by the death of Louis XIV. As long as Louis lived, Bolingbroke had some hope of drawing France into open hostility to England. " My hopes sunk as he declined, and died when he expired. He was the best friend the Chevalier had."

All chance of a Jacobite success even in Scotland depended on the Pretender's ability to secure an adequate supply of money and on French aid. The Duke of Berwick agreed fully with the views held by Bolingbroke and by Ormonde, who insisted that for success a large sum of money, artillery, and over 4,000 troops were required. Berwick, indeed, early in August conveyed to James Edward the unwelcome fact that matters could not be hurried on, though he had hopes that money and ships might soon be procured. The arrival of Ormonde in Paris on August the 6th was, however, a serious reminder that affairs in England were not progressing very favourably for the Jacobite cause. The death of Louis XIV. on September the 1st was a still more serious blow to the hopes of James Edward's supporter. Till that event took place there was always the possibility that French aid in men and money would be forthcoming, even though a rupture between England and France should be the consequence. No one could foretell what would happen in France when once the old King had passed away. The success of a Jacobite expedition depended, as Bolingbroke frequently asserted, on simultaneous risings in England and Scotland, on the presence of the Pretender in Scotland when his flag was unfurled, but chiefly on

French aid in troops, arms, and money. All hope of French assistance disappeared with the death of Louis XIV. His death, like that of Queen Anne, had come at a time most inopportune for the realization of Bolingbroke's plans, and from this time he lost the chief control of affairs. James Erskine, Earl of Mar, obeying orders transmitted to him, without Bolingbroke's knowledge, from James, raised the Pretender's standard at Braemar on September the 6th before all the Jacobite forces could be brought into the field. This rash act proved fatal to the cause of the Jacobites, for Orleans refused to give any aid, while the English Jacobites had already declared for a waiting policy. Any hope of a rising in England, however, was at an end before the beginning of November owing to the energetic measures of the English Government, while Admiral Byng at the head of an English squadron prevented any munitions of war from leaving Havre for Scotland. A rebel force did, indeed, march from Scotland to Preston, in Lancashire, only to suffer an overwhelming defeat at the hands of an English army. Early in November, at Sheriff Muir, a fiercely contested but undecisive battle was fought between Mar and Argyll, but the highland advance was checked, and from that time there was no unity of action by the supporters of the Pretender. In spite of the absence of any encouraging news, and undeterred by Ormonde's failure to effect a landing in Cornwall, James sailed from France, and landed at Peterhead on January the 2nd, 1716. His proclamation was not calculated to rouse enthusiasm, and the actual number of his troops did not exceed 5,000. Nevertheless, for a few weeks his cause was not thought to be desperate. Lord Mar persisted in his expectation of a rupture between France and England. On January the 31st Bolingbroke wrote a letter to Mar alluding to the early despatch of a ship with arms and ammunition to the west coast of Scotland, and lamenting that the Jacobite nobility and gentry in England have

8

no Duke of Mar to lead them.[1] But the Pretender's cause was already lost, and he was in some danger of capture by the English and Dutch troops. On February the 3rd, 1716, he wrote a somewhat despairing letter to the Regent Orleans, admitting that French help in men and money could alone save the situation. On February the 4th, having appointed General Alexander Gordon Commander-in-Chief of all his forces in Scotland, he embarked at Montrose with the Earl of Mar on board a French vessel, and arrived at Gravelines on February the 10th. The insurrection in Scotland was rapidly suppressed, and before the beginning of May order was restored, and the Jacobite movements, which never had any " national significance," ceased to interfere with the material progress of the country.

The return of the Pretender to France was followed by his dismissal of Bolingbroke from his service. Bolingbroke had made increasing efforts to secure the assistance of the Regent Orleans in furthering the Jacobite cause. He fully realized that without French help the rising in Scotland had no chance of success. In spite of Bolingbroke's untiring industry on behalf of the Jacobite cause, James Edward, shortly after his arrival in France, listened to the accusations of the rabble of St. Germain's, and dismissed him, his ablest supporter, from his post as Secretary. The blow to the Jacobite cause which James Edward thus inflicted was followed by another from the Regent Orleans the following month. The latter was already realizing that his position would be greatly strengthened by the establishment of good relations with England and Holland. His intimation to James Edward that his presence in France was inadvisable led the latter to leave Paris for Commercy on March the 7th, 1716, and to settle for a time at Avignon about April the 1st.

The reasons of James Edward's dismissal of Bolingbroke were various. The disappointment caused by the failure of

---

[1] Stuart Papers. Vol. I. Pp. 493, 494.

the expedition was no doubt the chief cause, for Bolingbroke refuted later the vague charges which were made against him of neglecting his duties. Berwick, at any rate, realized that his brother (the Pretender) had made an "enormous blunder in dismissing the only Englishman he had able to manage his affairs,"[1] and he expressed his appreciation of the value of Bolingbroke's services to the Jacobite cause :—

"I was, in fact, a witness," he wrote, "how Bolingbroke acted for King James whilst he managed his affairs, and I owe him the justice to say that he left nothing undone, of what he could do ; he moved heaven and earth to obtain supplies, but was always put off by the Court of France."

Lord Stair, writing to Horace Walpole, uses sarcastic language with regard to the Jacobite followers of the Pretender :—

"And so poor Harry is turned out from being Secretary of State, and the seals are given to Mar ; and they use poor Harry most unmercifully and call him knave and traitor, and God knows what. I believe all poor Harry's fault was that he could not play his part with a grave enough face ; he could not help laughing now and then at such kings and queens."

Bolingbroke was thus sacrificed to the jealousy of the crowd of miserable adventurers who surrounded the Chevalier ; and Berwick, the only other able man in James' service, recognized the real merit of the English statesman. His connection with the Jacobites was ended, and he attempted, through Lord Stair, to make terms with the English Government and to return to England. The news of his dismissal from the Pretender's service soon reached the Ministers, and it was not improbable that, in return for information about the strength and plans of the Jacobites, a pardon might be granted to the exiled statesman. In March, 1716, Stanhope, the Secretary-of-State, wrote to Stair, authorizing him to give Bolingbroke "all suitable hope and encouragement." In an interview with the Am-

[1] See Leadam, *The Political History of England*, 1702-1760. P. 263. London : Longmans.

bassador, Bolingbroke engaged to act loyally in the services of George I. and of England, to use all his efforts to induce those Tories who had embraced the Pretender's cause to return to their duty, but refused to turn informer. "To consent to betray private persons," he said, "or reveal secrets which may have been confided to me, would be to dishonour me for ever." Stair strongly advised the Ministers to restore Bolingbroke, and George declared himself favourable to his restoration, but the animosity of the Whigs, increased, perhaps, by his honourable refusal to damage his reputation by informing against individual Jacobites, resulted in a delay of some seven years.

In England, his father, Sir Henry St. John, was in 1716 created Baron of Battersea and Viscount St. John, and his wife was making vain attempts to regain her estate which had been confiscated when her husband was attainted. Though unable for state reasons to grant her request, George I. was certainly very favourably inclined towards Bolingbroke, and allowed his wife to retain a portion of the confiscated property. Bolingbroke himself wrote in September, 1716, a private letter to Wyndham, which was shown to Townshend, and in which the exiled statesman clearly demonstrated that he was cured of all Jacobite predilections. While he was kept in suspense, he returned to his literary studies; at the close of 1716 he wrote his *Reflections on Exile*, a close imitation of Seneca; in 1717 he dictated his celebrated *Letter to Sir William Wyndham*, describing the state of the Tory party during the last four years of Anne's reign, and his connection with the Jacobites in 1715. His object in writing it was partly to throw ridicule on the Jacobite cause, from which he was now dissevered, partly to point out to the English Tories the folly and uselessness of an alliance with the Jacobites. The immediate cause of this letter was the publication of a *Letter from Avignon* (written evidently with the Pretender's sanction), which had lately appeared, containing a reassertion of the charges of treachery and incapacity against Bolingbroke. Though, as Bolingbroke himself says, a medley of false facts, false arguments, and false eloquence, it had considerable effect, and required an answer. And in his overwhelming exposure of the Jacobites, in his amusing description of the St. Germain's rabble, and in his telling account of the characteristics of James, Bolingbroke ably defended his own conduct, and carried the war into the enemy's camp. This letter, which as a literary composition has been pronounced by a competent judge to be almost faultless, is, on the whole, fairly trustworthy. His account of the motives which induced him to join the Pretender is perhaps the only portion in which it is obviously impossible to place any confidence. This valuable addition to the secret history of the time was not published till 1753.

In 1717 Oxford was acquitted; in the next year Lady Bolingbroke died, and Bucklersbury passed to the representatives of her younger sister. From 1720 to 1723 he passed the greater part of his time on the small estate of La Source, which he had bought with some money he had made in the early days of the Great Mississippi Scheme. La Source was situated near Orleans, and took its name from the sudden rise of the Loiret in the grounds. Pope, in a letter to Bolingbroke, enclosed the following lines :

> " What pleasing frenzy steals away my soul ?
>   Through thy blest shades, La Source, I seem to rove ;
>   I see thy fountains fall, thy waters roll,
>   And breathe the zephyrs that refresh thy grove ;
>   I hear whatever can delight inspire,
>   Villette's soft voice and St. John's silver lyre."

In this quiet retreat he devoted himself, as he had done at Bucklersbury, between the years 1708 and 1710, to historical and philosophical studies, which led him to write the *Letters to M. de Pouilly.* He corresponded with Swift, and in July, 1721, tried in vain to induce him to visit France. Among his visitors was Voltaire, who at the end of 1721 began a friendship with Bolingbroke which was to have important results on France and Europe. Voltaire was delighted with his visit.

"I have found," he wrote to a friend, "in this eminent Englishman all the learning of his country and all the politeness of ours. . . . This man, who has been all his life immersed in pleasure and business, has, however, found time for learning everything and retaining everything. He is as well acquainted with the history of the ancient Egyptians as with that of England. He knows Virgil as well as Milton. He loves the poetry of England, France, and Italy ; but he loves them differently, because he discerns perfectly the difference of their genius."

In 1722 Bolingbroke's marriage with Marie Claire, Marquise de Villette, a niece of Madame de Maintenon, took place at Aix-la-Chapelle. Since 1717 they had met both in Paris and at her mansion of Marcilly. Her devotion to Bolingbroke continued till her death, and though her delicate constitution resented the English climate, she paid frequent visits to England. Her death in 1751 was probably the most serious blow that he ever sustained. At the time of his second marriage Bolingbroke was far from being contented with his retired life. He longed to be in England. He begged Orleans and Dubois to advocate his cause with the English Government ; he applied directly and frequently to the English Ministers. Polwarth and Stair interested themselves in his behalf, and Townshend and Carteret used their influence with the King. At last, early in 1723, his pardon passed the Great Seal, though the Act of Attainder still remained in force.

In June he paid a short visit to London, meeting Atterbury, who had just been banished, at Dover. That prelate, who was no longer on good terms with Bolingbroke, is reported to have exclaimed, " I am exchanged !"

In England Walpole had risen on the ruins of Sunderland's commercial policy, and in 1721 that famous Ministry which was to reconcile the English nation to the Hanoverian dynasty had taken office. Walpole and Townshend, though supreme in Parliament, found their position already imperilled by the influence of their colleague Carteret, whose knowledge of German, and sympathy with the Hanoverian policy seemed likely to make him a great favourite with George. It was impossible for the Ministry to contain both Walpole and Carteret. It appeared as though the Court with Carteret would be pitted against Walpole and the Parliament. Here, then, was a splendid field for Bolingbroke, whose object in returning to England was to secure the reversal of the attainder, and his complete restoration to political life. It was soon evident to him that Carteret's star was waning, and that Walpole's ascendancy was assured. He therefore opened negotiations for an alliance between the Whigs and the Hanoverian Tories, promising that the latter, now weary of opposition, would heartily support the Government. He saw that in such a union, bringing with it reconciliation with Walpole, lay his only chance of procuring his complete restoration. But the Whigs had already declared plainly they would have nothing to say to a union with the Tories. They viewed with great displeasure Bolingbroke's pardon. " I am sorry," wrote Townshend to Walpole in July, 1723, " to find Lord Bolingbroke's affair continues to make ill blood among our friends." The attitude of the Whig party only confirmed the Ministers in their determination to refuse all offers of a Tory alliance, and Walpole promptly declined to consider Bolingbroke's overtures for a Coalition, and told him he had done a most imprudent thing in negotiating to bring in a set of Tories when his salvation depended on a Whig Parliament.

Though he had failed to attain the main object of his visit, Bolingbroke had the pleasure of seeing his old friends, Wyndham and Harcourt, and of making some new ones in Lord Finch and the Earl of Berkeley, the former being the son of Lord Nottingham. Until his attainder was reversed there was no reason for a long stay in England, and in September he set out for Aix-la-Chapelle. His ill health was the ostensible object of this journey, but there is little doubt that he hoped to procure an interview with George I. at Herrenhausen and to plead his cause in person. Receiving no invitation to go to Hanover, he returned to Paris, and found the diplomatic struggle between Townshend and Carteret at its height. The position of the Ministry was as yet far from being assured. While in Hanover with George I. in 1723 Townshend was busily engaged in combating the influence of Carteret. The latter had, in fact, staked all upon his success in procuring a Dukedom for the father of a young French count, who was about to marry a daughter of Madame de Platen, sister to the King's mistress, the Countess of Darlington. Hitherto Carteret's influence in Paris had been great: the Regent and Dubois were his friends, Sir Luke Schaub, the English Ambassador, was his nominee.

But on Bolingbroke's arrival at Paris at the beginning of the winter of 1723-4 he found important changes had taken place. Dubois and Orleans were both dead. The Duke of Bourbon had become First Minister, and Horace Walpole, the nominee of Townshend and Walpole, had practically superseded Schaub. It was clear that, if Carteret failed, his influence was gone. To Townshend it was all-important he should fail. Into this struggle, occurring, as it did, at a moment when the relations between England and France consequent on the death of Orleans were uncertain, Bolingbroke threw himself; he supported Horace Walpole, and undertook to influence Bourbon to reject Carteret's demand. It was a matter of no little difficulty for Horace Walpole, who, however, made considerable use of Bolingbroke's information to prevent the latter from taking the complete lead in the diplomatic intrigue. In this affair Bolingbroke worked with all his old energy and as hard as in the days when he was Secretary of State. But, beyond irritating Carteret, his labours had no immediate reward, though Townshend in 1723 had assured him of George I.'s goodwill. After remaining some time at Paris, and consorting frequently with the French philosophers at the Entresol Club, established by the Abbé Alari, and supported by such men as Count d'Argenson and the Abbé Charles St. Pierre, Bolingbroke was in the summer of 1724 again at La Source and still under the Act of Attainder. In May Lady Bolingbroke went to England for a second time, and strengthened her husband's chances by sending to the Duchess of Kendal a large bribe. Many friends, such as the Abbé Alari, Finch, and more especially Harcourt, exerted themselves on his behalf, but it was not till May, 1725, partly owing to the efforts of Sir Philip Yorke, the Attorney-General, who, though a member of the Government, spoke in favour of the measure,[1] that a Bill passed enabling Bolingbroke to enjoy his family estates, and to inherit landed property in England. The other provisions of the Act of Attainder remained in force, preventing him rom sitting in either House of Parliament and from holding any place of trust under the Crown. His exile was now over, and he was at liberty to return to England, and live on his property. He was, as he wrote somewhat sarcastically from London to Swift,—

"tired with suspense, the only insupportable misfortune of life, and with nine years of autumnal promises and vernal excuses. . . . Here I am, then," he continued, "two-thirds restored, my person safe (unless I meet hereafter with harder treatment than even that of Sir Walter Raleigh), and my estate, with all the other property I have acquired or may acquire, secured to me. But the attainder is kept carefully and prudently in force, lest so corrupt a member should come again into the House of Lords, and his bad leaven should sour that sweet, untainted mass."

---

[1] *Life and Correspondence of Philip Yorke, Earl of Hardwicke, Lord High Chancellor of Great Britain*, by Philip Yorke. Vol. I., p. 97. Cambridge : at the University Press, 1913.

CHAPTER VI

THE OPPOSITION TO WALPOLE.

1725-1742.

ON his return to England, Bolingbroke lived partly on an
estate called Dawley, near Uxbridge, which he had bought
from Lord Tankerville, partly in his house in Pall Mall.
At Dawley he again became the centre of a brilliant literary

society; when in London, he threw himself heart and soul into the midst of one of the most exciting political struggles ever seen in this country. He had been absent from England some nine years. During those years the Whig party had experienced strange vicissitudes. The accession of George found the Whigs a united minority; the suppression of the rebellion of 1715 strengthened their position incalculably. Till 1745 the stigma of Jacobitism lay on the Tories, and all the efforts of Bolingbroke failed to assure the King and people that a Tory Government would not lead to the subversion of the dynasty. Ministerial influence at elections, combined with Tory apathy and the Septennial Act, all helped to place the Whig party in an almost impregnable position. In carrying out their policy, the exile of Bolingbroke had been of the utmost importance to the Whigs. He, and he alone, could have reconciled the great Tory party to the Hanoverian dynasty. His absence enabled the Whigs to establish firmly their power on a secure basis, and to govern England till 1760. Their immediate objects were to establish firmly the Hanoverian dynasty on the throne, to destroy all chance of another Jacobite rebellion, and to advance the interests of the commercial classes. Peace with France became the keystone of their policy, for no Jacobite rebellion had any chance of success without French aid. Hence the Treaty of Utrecht, followed by the Triple Alliance of 1717, were of enormous value to the Whig party. They were enabled to consolidate their own power, to increase the wealth and prosperity of all classes, and to reconcile the nation to the new dynasty so thoroughly, that, when hostilities between England and France were renewed in the war of The Austrian Succession, the Jacobite Rising of '45 never for a moment endangered the throne of George II. The Whig Schism of 1717, and the collapse of the South Sea Scheme in no way impaired the real strength of the Whig party; and in 1725 Bolingbroke found the Tories reduced to complete powerlessness through the imputation of Jacobitism, and a united Whig Ministry in office under Walpole and Townshend. He was under no obligation whatever to Walpole, and seeing that many Whigs were hostile to him on personal grounds, he joined with Pulteney in 1726 in a celebrated attack on the Whig Government. Till 1735 Bolingbroke was the mainspring of a powerful Opposition to Walpole. To comprehend the real meaning of his political writings and the importance and objects of this Opposition, which he was mainly instrumental in forming, it is necessary to realize the position of Walpole, and the true tendency of his policy.

It will be remembered that Bolingbroke's aim during the four last years of Anne's troubled reign was to restore the Church and the Tory landed interest to the position they occupied in the Government of England before the Revolution. He wished, in fact, to undo in great part the Revolution Settlement, and by means of a system of thorough party consolidation to establish Toryism on a firm basis. Oxford's love of compromise and his hatred of a policy of " thorough," together with Anne's death, ruined Bolingbroke's plan. With the accession of George, the Revolution Settlement was assured, the Parliamentary triumphed over the Monarchical system, and it became the policy of the Whigs to prevent all chance of a return to the Tory principles of Anne's reign. Their Government, resting on the support of the Nonconformists and of the middle and commercial class—that "moneyed interest," which was so unpopular with the Tory country gentlemen —aimed at overthrowing the influence and power of the Church and the Tories. The immense effect of the Sacheverell episode on the elections of 1710 and 1713 had not been forgotten. " The Church in Danger " was a cry which the Whigs had good reason to dread. Before Walpole had been many years in office, the blighting influence of the Whig oligarchy had fallen heavily on the Church. Convocation had been suppressed for many years, and in 1717 all ecclesiastical appointments were given to staunch Whigs. Walpole and his party were directly answerable for the lifeless Christianity which prevailed during two-thirds of the eighteenth century, for the absence of Church development and for the rapid deterioration in the whole tone of Churchmen, and that at a time when the increasing interest in commercial pursuits, and the growth of population at home and in our colonies, rendered the extension of Church organization of paramount importance. By means of bribery and patronage, Walpole succeeded in carrying out a policy which, if openly advocated, would have been vehemently resisted.

The specious attack on the Church by the Whigs had inflicted a severe blow at the political principles of the Tories ; party organization, which Bolingbroke had so earnestly tried to establish, completed their overthrow. Walpole's policy throughout was to secure the Government of the country in the hands of a body of aristo-cratic statesmen by means of "an extended system of Parliamentary influence," and during his long tenure of power he succeeded in this policy. The Church and the Tory landed interest—these two features of the old constitution which had under Bolingbroke so nearly regained their former predominance—were suppressed, and the whole government answerable to the Prime Minister, became vested in the hands of the Revolution families, who were, generally speaking, independent alike of the King and of the people. According to the Whig view, the Government of England should be in the hands of Parliament ; while Parliament, in which was collected all men of wealth, position, and intelligence, should be strong enough to resist the influence of the Crown and the violence of the people. The nation, it was thought, would readily acquiesce, seeing that the Whigs secured for them civil and religious liberty, free Parliamentary institutions, and commercial advantages, and at the same time defended them from the authority of the Crown, the ascendancy of the Church, and the exclusive policy of the Tory country gentlemen.

Such was the Whig plan of Government, ostensibly designed to make the will of the nation, as expressed in Parliament, supreme, but which, when put into execution, developed many defects of a startling description, defects which were boldly seized upon by a powerful Opposition led by Bolingbroke and Pulteney. The advantages of Parliamentary Government were not so obvious to men of Walpole's day as they perhaps are to modern statesmen. To secure the Ministry from defeat, Walpole, partly by means of corruption, organized a powerful Whig majority. His knowledge of the wants of the nation, and his usual deference to public opinion enabled him to avoid the introduction of unpopular measures. The result of his foresight and clever management was that he remained in power for twenty years, during which period he consolidated Parliamentary Government, fixed it on party lines, and made the Executive Government practically responsible to Parliament. But, even during his tenure of office, there were signs that, though the Whig oligarchy governed with remarkable party success and with benefit to the " moneyed " class, Parliament was ceasing to represent the nation, and was becoming an assembly of the nominees of the great Whig families. The shameless system of corruption, the absence of high qualities in Walpole himself, the personal hatred of the Minister by the great body of Malcontent Whigs, his policy of repression, exclusion, and proscription, the growing indignation at his peace-at-any-price policy, the unpopularity of the Excise Scheme, all contributed to weaken his position, and eventually caused his fall. But, before he fell, he had succeeded in establishing the Hanoverian dynasty firmly on the throne, he had given the nation a long period of peace, during which the material prosperity increased in a marvellous degree, he had seen the final triumph of the Parliamentary over the Monarchical system, and of the Revolution over the policy which Bolingbroke attempted to carry out during Queen Anne's last years.

Bolingbroke, it has been said, was under no obligation to Walpole. It would be true to say he had every reason to seize the first opportunity of revenging himself on a Minister, who had withheld his readmission to Parliament, and doomed him to lifelong exclusion from Parliamentary life.

His first step was characteristic. By the aid of the Duchess of Kendal, he succeeded in obtaining an interview with the King. The interview was a failure; George at that moment was not prepared to get rid of a Minister who suited him in many ways in order to try constitutional experiments under Bolingbroke's guidance. There was, however, always the possibility, which Walpole himself recognized, that the influence of the Duchess of Kendal would prevail, and that Bolingbroke's star would again be in the ascendant. Defeated in his first attempt to undermine the Minister, Bolingbroke turned to Leicester House, where the Prince of Wales lived at open enmity with his father. By means of Mrs. Howard, who afterwards became Lady Suffolk, he hoped to ingratiate himself at Leicester House, and at once began to weave plans for the formation of a " Patriotic " Ministry, with Chesterfield, who then stood high in the favour of the Prince. Again he was doomed to disappointment. George II. succeeded his father in June, 1727, and Walpole retired in favour of Sir Spencer Compton. But any hopes entertained by Bolingbroke were soon dispelled, and after an interval of a few days, Walpole was again firmly established in power, and Bolingbroke fell back on a scheme which he had already evolved, and which, though eventually successful in overthrowing Walpole, did not result in his own return to Parliamentary life.

This scheme simply consisted of bringing together all the men who, from various causes, either regarded Walpole with hatred or disliked his policy from principle, and of uniting these scattered elements into one body. Bolingbroke's rare abilities, his knowledge of the world and of men rendered him peculiarly well fitted for this self-imposed task, and between the years 1726 and 1735 he was largely instrumental in forming that famous Opposition which, after sixteen years of persistent party warfare, succeeded in overthrowing the great Peace Minister. Walpole's jealousy of any possible rival, his system of party exclusiveness, and his government by patronage had alienated a large section of the Whigs, which included in their ranks William and Daniel Pulteney, and a few years later Carteret. Of these men, William Pulteney was at that time the most distinguished. To the advantages of birth and wealth he had united a remarkable acquaintance with ancient and modern literature. He was an incisive writer of telling pamphlets; he was a brilliant debater. No such orator was seen in the House of Commons between the fall of Bolingbroke and the rise of Chatham. His brilliancy and versatility naturally gave him the position of leader of the Malcontent Whigs. And he had reasons for his discontent. Hitherto a consistent Whig, he had retired with Walpole in 1717, throwing up a valuable appointment. When Walpole returned to power, Pulteney, instead of receiving a seat in the Cabinet, was given a post in the household, and was offered a Peerage. It was not, however, till April, 1725, that Pulteney found himself unable to support Walpole any longer. From that moment he resolved to revenge himself on the Minister who had wronged him. In spite of his lack of statesmanlike qualities, and his want of judgment and of method, in spite of his restless and impetuous character, William Pulteney became one of the most prominent members of the Opposition to Walpole. His brother Daniel, whose energy and debating powers were also very considerable, brought to the assistance of the opponents of Walpole very useful, business-like qualities, and an animosity to the Whig Minister, which roused all the activity of his nature. Personal dislike, then, and resentment at real or supposed wrongs had caused this revolt of the Malcontent Whigs. Opposed to the Minister on almost every subject save that of the Succession was the large body of Constitutional or Hanoverian Tories, led by Sir William Wyndham, an upright man, with great oratorical gifts and a high reputation for statesmanship. About fifty Jacobites under Shippen were ready to attack the Government on any subject, while the best known literary names were also found ranged in antagonism to the Minister. All the surviving members of the Scriblerus Club sided with Bolingbroke, and were reinforced by such men as Johnson and Fielding, Thomson and Akenside.

During his tenure of office, from 1710 to 1714, Bolingbroke had displayed great presence of mind, extraordinary skill in unravelling the involved interests of the various European Powers, and a firmness and determination which, unfettered, would have saved the Tory party from their overthrow on Anne's death. He now showed an unexpected capacity for organization, and there is no doubt that it was entirely to his genius, to his knowledge of political strategy, to his vast intellectual abilities, that the three sections of Jacobites, Hanoverian Tories, and Malcontent Whigs were welded into that famous Coalition which, embracing as it did, most of the political and literary talent of the day, finally succeeded in overthrowing Walpole. In 1725 Bolingbroke and Pulteney agreed to unite. On December the 5th, 1726, appeared the first number of *The Craftsman*, with Caleb d'Anvers of Gray's Inn as nominal editor, but which was really founded by Pulteney and was under his and Bolingbroke's management. From December the 5th, 1726, to April the 17th, 1736, this weekly paper thundered against Walpole.

In 1737 all the papers were published in a collected form in fourteen volumes. Of these, Volumes I. to VII. deal principally with England's connection with foreign countries between 1726 and April, 1731, when that Second Treaty of Vienna was signed, which weakened our close alliance with France, reconciled France and Spain, and partly led to the combined Bourbon attack, in 1733, upon the Emperor on the Rhine and in Italy. Volumes VIII. to XIV. are mainly concerned with the domestic Government of Walpole between May, 1731, and April the 17th, 1736. This division is by no means absolutely accurate, as domestic policy is sometimes treated of in Vols. I. to VII., and foreign policy is at times criticized in Vols. VIII. to XIV. The papers usually attributed to Pulteney are marked C; those written by Bolingbroke are usually marked O. Of the latter the most important are published in Bolingbroke's Collected Works, and are fine specimens of the best political and controversial writing of the day. Other contributors would seem to have been Amherst, Arbuthnot, Swift, and probably Pope. If we remember how at that time political influence was confined to the classes who read good literature, we shall not feel any surprise at the extraordinary influence wielded by *The Craftsman*, and the importance attached even by Walpole to its utterances.

The Conduct of the Allies had shown people the real meaning of the Spanish Succession War in its later stages; *The Craftsman* played an equally important part in pointing out to the nation the faults of Walpole's administration, and in forming a public opinion hostile to that Minister.

On all points of home and foreign policy Walpole found himself attacked. In the *First Vision of Camelick*, written in *The Craftsman* early in 1727, Bolingbroke, in a most excellent specimen of satirical writing, attacks Walpole's tyranny, corruption, and contempt for the Constitution. In a dream which he dreamed in Bagdad, Walpole is represented as—

"a man dressed in a plain habit, with a purse of gold in his hand. He threw himself forward into the room in a bluff, ruffianly manner, a smile or rather a sneer sat on his countenance. His face was bronzed over with a glare of confidence, an arch malignity leered in his eye. Nothing was so extraordinary as the effect of this person's appearance. They no sooner saw him, but they all turned their faces from the canopy, and fell prostrate before him. He trod over their backs without any ceremony, and marched directly up to the throne. He opened his purse of gold, which he took out in handfuls, and scattered amongst the assembly. Whilst the greater part were engaged in scrambling for these pieces, he seized, to my inexpressible surprise, without the least fear, upon the sacred parchment itself. He rumpled it rudely up and crammed it into his pocket. Some of the people began to murmur ; he threw more gold, and they were pacified. No sooner was the parchment taken, but in an instant I saw half the august assembly in chains. Nothing was heard through the whole divan but the noise of fetters and the clank of iron."

Bolingbroke then described how Walpole, as soon as his purse was empty, lost all his influence, how the sacred volume again assumed its place above the throne, how the throne itself was lightened, how every chain fell off, and how the heart of the king was glad within him.

In this paper Bolingbroke took up the position which he afterwards developed—namely, that Walpole's system of Government was really a violation of the Constitution, and that the new power of Parliament bringing with it the loss of freedom at elections, and a fresh form of bribery in the shape of places and pensions, was a disastrous innovation. This special danger he pointed out in his *Three Letters on the History of Athens*, published in *The Craftsman* in 1732 and designed to prove that corruption destroyed the Athenian State. The example of Pericles is cited to show how the overgrown power, ambition, and corruption of one man brought ruin upon the most flourishing State in the universe.

In his *Remarks on the History of England*, written in *The Craftsman* in 1730 and 1731, under the signature of Humphrey Oldcastle, he boldly attacked Walpole and his whole system of Government. These letters are an attempt to convey " satire under the form of analogue," and in them Bolingbroke tries to make the history of past times the counterpart of the present. Their popularity was due, not only to the brilliant style in which they were written, but also to the skill with which Walpole and his Government were attacked. The characteristics of a bad Minister were exemplified in the cases of de Vere, Suffolk, Wolsey, and Buckingham. These letters are well worthy of perusal as a remarkable indictment against Revolution principles as developed by Walpole, and are written with a brilliancy and eloquence rarely surpassed. In his concluding (the twenty-fourth) letter Bolingbroke defends his own conduct against the attacks of Ministerial writers. He declares that he never projected nor procured the disgrace of Harley, that he never joined the Jacobite cause till after his attainder, and that, while grateful to George I., he was under no obligation to Walpole.

Other writers in *The Craftsman* were hardly less vigorous. In No. 51, which appeared on June the 24th, 1727, and which is a good illustration of the kind of attack to which Walpole was subjected, the marks of a bad Administration were declared to be—*first*, the dread of examination and the constant endeavour of men in power to keep their actions in the dark ; *secondly*, the use of unwarrantable methods to influence the Members, or to impair the freedom of Senates or of popular assemblies ; *thirdly*, the general encouragement of luxury ; *fourthly*, pretended plots and rebellions ; *fifthly*, forging or suborning evidence and packing juries; *sixthly*, the conferring of principal offices of State on members of one family or tribe, and the lesser places on worthless wretches and tools of known incapacity; *lastly*, the endeavour of Ministers to thrust the odium of their unpopular actions on their royal master.

Nor were the attacks on Walpole confined to prose. On July the 20th, 1728, appeared a sarcastic poem, entitled, *The Norfolk Lanthorn*, of which these verses are appended:

> " In the county of Norfolk, that Paradise land,
> Whose riches and power doth all Europe command,
> There stands a great House (and long may it stand),
> Which nobody can deny.

> " And in this great House there is a great Hall,
> So spacious it is, and so sumptuous withal,
> It excells Master Wolsey's Hampton Court and Whitehall,
> Which nobody can deny.

> " To adorn this great Room both by day and by night,
> And convince all the world that the deeds of Sir Knight
> Stand in need of no darkness, there hangs a great Light,
> Which nobody can deny."

While *The Craftsman* poured in invective after invective on all points of Walpole's domestic policy, on the Septennial Act, standing armies, loss of liberty at elections, absolute Ministers, and favourites, the foreign policy of the Government did not escape. In consequence of a very ill-advised letter which George I. had some years previously sent to the King of Spain, it was believed that the Ministers intended to restore Gibraltar to Spain. A storm of indignation was provoked, and a complete renunciation by Spain of any claim to Gibraltar was demanded. In March, April, and May of 1727, this question was taken up in some very forcible papers which appeared in *The Craftsman*. England, it was asserted, had obtained Gibraltar in open war, and its cession by the Treaty of Utrecht had been again confirmed by the Quadruple Alliance. Any promise of restitution was only a Ministerial promise, and therefore not binding. Besides, it was the only valuable benefit we gained by the Spanish Succession War. Its importance to English trade was immense. On its possession depended our Italian and Turkish trade, and by means of it we were enabled to check the Algerine pirates and to compete with the French trade from Marseilles. Then, again, it had a great military value. The connection between the French and Spanish ports could be checked, the power of the French fleet was practically destroyed, and the trade between Cadiz and the West Indies was commanded. Therefore, concluded *The Craftsman,* the possession of Gibraltar is important, from a political no less than from a military point of view.

No one at the present day will deny the justice of these criticisms. But there was little proof that Walpole ever intended to give up Gibraltar, though there is evidence that both George I. and George II. were not unwilling to consider the question of its restitution. Less justifiable was another well-known attack on the Whig conduct of foreign affairs. A capital subject for invective was found in the non-fulfilment of the terms of the Peace of Utrecht with regard to the demolition of the harbour of Dunkirk, and numerous papers were written in *The Craftsman* on this matter between 1727 and 1731. In July, 1728, it even went so far as to assert that "even the restitution of Gibraltar would be of much less fatal consequence on Great Britain than the reparation of Dunkirk." It must not, however, be supposed that the Government did not resent the criticisms which were levelled at its policy by *The Craftsman.* In February, 1729, Sir Philip Yorke, the Attorney-General, who had joined the Ministry in 1724 and was always on good terms with Bolingbroke, on behalf of the Government, failed in a prosecution for libel against Francklin, the printer and publisher, with the result that a ballad, inscribed to Pulteney and styled *The Honest Jury, or Caleb Triumphant,* appeared and acquired great popularity. However, on the appearance on January the 2nd, 1731, of a *Letter from the Hague*, ascribed to Bolingbroke and accusing the Ministers of perfidy towards their Allies, the Government won, and Francklin was fined and imprisoned.[1]   On October the 14th, 1731, appeared a *New Court Ballad*, of which the third verse runs as follows :

> " About Dunkirk and Gib
> Some tongues run very glib
> And offer us to lay a round sum, sum, sum,
> That Spain means this or that
> And France, the Lord knows what :
> But still shall old Caleb be dumb, dumb, dumb."

In fact, all through the ten years in which *The Craftsman* appeared, numerous attacks were made on Walpole's Peace Policy, on the Porto Bello Expedition, and on the Treaty of Hanover, on the Minister's alienation from the Austrians by the Treaty of Seville in 1729, when Spain, disgusted at the evident faithlessness of the Emperor, Charles VI., in the matter of the Italian Duchies, found her best policy in alliance with England and France. Walpole's conclusion of the Second Treaty of Vienna in 1731 with Spain and Austria was also attacked, by which Treaty Charles VI., yielding to the bribe of the English guarantee of the Pragmatic Sanction, agreed to withdraw all opposition to the claims of Spain on the Duchies ; and finally his disregard of the growing power of the Bourbons, and his consequent neglect of the pressing needs of the mercantile interest was severely criticized. It was with reference to the danger to Europe from Bourbon aggrandizement, that in March and April, 1736, appeared four letters, attributed to Bolingbroke, in which the preliminaries of the final Peace of Vienna were forcibly censured. The cession of Lorraine and Bar to

---

[1] *Life and Correspondence of Philip Yorke, Earl of Hardwicke, Lord High Chancellor of England*, by Philip Yorke. Vol. I., pp. 82-86. Cambridge : at the University Press, 1913.

France, and of the Tuscan ports to any member of the Bourbon House was, the writer contended, strongly to be deprecated. The French would thus secure a connection with Naples and an opening into the middle of Italy, the growth of Savoy would be checked, and England's trade endangered. This protest was unavailing; England had remained at peace during the Polish Succession War (1733-38), and by the Final Treaty of Vienna in 1738 France secured Lorraine and Bar, Don Carlos obtained Naples, Sicily, and the Tuscan ports, and Austria, England's old ally, though she obtained Parma and Piacenza, came out of the struggle considerably weakened.

Till 1735 Bolingbroke never relaxed his efforts. He directed from outside all Wyndham's eloquent onslaughts in the House of Commons, and settled on the policy to be followed by the Parliamentary Opposition. He had violently attacked Walpole, not only in *The Craftsman*, but also in three papers, known as *The Occasional Writer*, which appeared independently of *The Craftsman*, and which are remarkable for their violence, even in days when acrimonious and personal attacks were of common occurrence. At length the Opposition were convinced that, in the unpopularity of Walpole's Excise Scheme, they had found certain means of overthrowing the Ministry. *The Craftsman* became the more violent, as it was thought that Walpole's power was shaken. In *No.* 348 it inveighed against "the oppressions, insolences, and unjustifiable partialities of the Commissioners of Excise." It pointed out that the Excise system in Holland and Venice was less oppressive than it would be in England, while in *No.* 353 it compared the situation to that of 1627, when it asserted that there was a design on foot for enslaving the nation by means of Excises and a standing army. On this occasion *The Craftsman*, representing the ignorance of the mass of Englishmen in matters of political economy, found that its views received very considerable support. The members of the Government were not united on the question, and it was clear that the stability of the Ministry would be endangered if the scheme was persevered with. Walpole bowed before the storm, withdrew the Excise Bill, and then took decided measures against his disaffected followers. Chesterfield, Stair, Cobham, and others were at once dismissed from their respective posts, and joined the ranks of the Opposition. On April the 28th, 1733, *No.* 356 of *The Craftsman* expressed the satisfaction of the Opposition at the withdrawal of the Excise Bill. " We have seen an insolent domineering Minister reduced, after all his defiances, to the wretched necessity of recanting his abusive reflections and giving up his infamous projects."

This victory over Walpole, however, hardly redounds to the credit of Bolingbroke. He had been forced in 1713, in deference to the ignorant prejudices of his age, to withdraw his great Commercial Treaty with France. We find him now, instead of sympathizing with Walpole's enlightened economical views, opposing the Excise Bill, not, it is true, on economic, but on political, grounds. In spite of some economic advantages which, he allowed, would attend the measure, he advocated uncompromising opposition, on the ground that the scheme was a mere electioneering stratagem on the part of Walpole, who saw in the extension of the Excise system fresh opportunities for increasing the number of Whig revenue officers, placemen, and election agents. Hence, he argued, the liberties of the nation, which were already endangered by Walpole's tenure of office, would be still more imperilled were the Excise Bill to become law.

It was now hoped that at the ensuing elections the voters would testify their sense of the conduct of the Whig Minister, and reject his candidates at the polling booths. Bolingbroke, therefore, redoubled his attacks on Walpole. In the autumn of 1733 he began in the pages of *The Craftsman* a series of nineteen letters entitled a *Dissertation on Parties*. These letters, which when published in a collected form were dedicated to Walpole, contained an elaborate attack on that Minister's administration, and, written between October, 1733, and December, 1734, had by 1737 passed through two editions. *The Dissertation on Parties* remains the most complete indictment against Walpole's policy as well as one of the most brilliant of the political pamphlets of the eighteenth century. Bolingbroke's object in these letters was twofold. He wished not only to weaken Walpole's position on the eve of the general election, but also to heal the differences between the various sections of the Opposition. Of these sections the Malcontent Whigs were the most unmanageable. It was in order to unite these Malcontent Whigs more firmly to the Tory and Jacobite sections of the Opposition that Bolingbroke in these letters vindicates the principles established at the Revolution Settlement, inveighs against the party system with its party prejudices, and contends that Walpole, to serve his own personal ends, had revived bygone distinctions and obsolete party divisions. To the nation he appealed on behalf of the patriotic Opposition, which, he declared, was defending the true principles of the Revolution.

The elections of 1734 were held amid the greatest excitement. The Government had been guilty of many mistakes; it was notorious for its corruption; it was in reality not popular with the country at large. Though the Tories were returned in many county constituencies, notably for Gloucestershire which had been Whig since 1688, the overwhelming borough interest of the Whigs secured for Walpole a majority, though a diminished one. Thus the efforts of Bolingbroke, Pulteney, and their followers were for the time in vain. The violent attacks on, and the elaborate indictments of Walpole's policy had failed for the time to effect their object. A few years later, when the nation was discontented and less prosperous, Bolingbroke's controversial writings contributed in great measure to the overthow of the Whig Minister. For the present the Opposition had to acquiesce in the defeat of their great attempt to oust from power the established Government. The returns had shown that Walpole's influence in the country was still strong, and the nation, as Bolingbroke said, preferred, like a patient, to bear his "constitutional malady than to undergo the remedies prescribed by his physician." Walpole's majority was certainly diminished, but only to a small extent, and five years were yet to elapse before his Administration would be seriously threatened.

The paper warfare, however, continued with the same violence. On May the 25th, just after the elections, *The Craftsman* attacked the various methods taken by the favourites of power to secure their own election and that of their creatures. The writer boasts that the counties have gone against the Government, and that the Ministers owe their majority to the little boroughs. He then attacks the votes of Custom-house and Excise Officers, and hopes the members of Parliament will not be the tools of a desperate Minister. On June the 1st *The Craftsman* alluded to Walpole as a corrupt Minister, corrupting the people and thus destroying the effects of a good Constitution. The writer compares the state of England with that of the Roman Empire under Tiberius, and regrets that George II. disdains to use his power. Though, however, *The Craftsman* continued to thunder against Walpole till 1737, Bolingbroke had for some time ceased to take a leading part in its management.

In 1735 his political connection with Pulteney came to an end, and he retired to France. The Opposition to Walpole continued, but Bolingbroke no longer led it. With his departure, the principles which had been the basis of the Coalition disappeared, and the struggle deteriorated into a mere contest between the Whigs out of office and the Whigs in office.

In forming the celebrated Coalition of Malcontent Whigs, Jacobites, and Tories, Bolingbroke had intended that it should ostensibly support the Revolution principles against a Minister who, he asserted, had frequently violated those principles. A supreme Cabinet, the division of Parliament into parties, the diminution of the King's power, the rise of the modern First Minister, were all, in Bolingbroke's eyes, dangerous innovations. He asserted that the Revolution Settlement did not naturally lead to the impotence of the King, nor to the development of Parliament from a consulting, heterogeneous body, presided over by the King, into a powerful administrative body which, under the leadership of one man chosen by the majority, really governed.

There was nothing in the old Whig traditions which called upon Pulteney and his followers to reject Bolingbroke's view of Walpole's system of Government. There was no reason why the Opposition should not be a " union and coalition of parties meeting together on a national bottom." But, though Bolingbroke had formed out of a number of discontented sections, united merely by personal dislike of Walpole and by a desire to avenge personal grievances, a powerful Opposition with a valuable literary organ and definite constitutional watchwords, he never really secured the hearty support of the Malcontent Whigs. They were delighted to make use of his intellectual abilities, and of his extraordinary versatility; they were perfectly willing to accept his definition of Constitutional Government; they even consented to unite with the Jacobite section in attacking a common enemy; but the ultimate aim of their policy differed widely from that of Bolingbroke. To Bolingbroke the opposition :—

"is not an opposition only to a bad administration of public affairs, but to an administration that supports itself by means, establishes principles, introduces customs, repugnant to the constitution of our Government and destructive of all liberty." In his letter on the *Spirit of Patriotism*, which he wrote to Lord Lyttelton, is the following sentence : " You owe to your country, to your honour, to your security, to the present and to future ages, that no endeavour of yours be wanting to repair the breach that is made, and is increasing daily in the Constitution."

But Bolingbroke's efforts to raise the opposition to Walpole into something higher than a mere struggle for place ended in failure. He had appealed principally to the large body of Malcontent Whigs. They had rebelled against Walpole's personal authority, not against his system of Government. They were willing to use any weapons, any cries, to oust him from power, but they were in complete sympathy with his scheme of party Government. They had no reverence for the monarch, they lacked the historical spirit, they dreaded all display of Church feeling, they had no sympathy with popular aspirations. The Whigs were ever the same. Exclusive, and self-seeking, they were always ready to sacrifice all principles of political morality to secure the possession of power. In order to drive Walpole out of office, Pulteney and his friends were willing to make use of Bolingbroke's exertions, though they disagreed with his principles, and even to make an alliance, essentially immoral, with the Jacobites. So, in 1783, the Whigs, under Fox, formed with North and the Tories the famous Coalition Ministry, and were rewarded for their disregard of political morality by practical exclusion from power for nearly fifty years.

Bolingbroke had, it appears, taken the measure of his Whig supporters before 1735. In 1733 he had written to Pope :—

"Disarmed, gagged, and almost bound as I am, I shall continue in the drudgery of public business only so long as the integrity and perseverance of the men who, with none of my disadvantages, are co-operating with me, make it reasonable to me to engage in it."

In 1734, the Malcontent Whigs had shown unmistakably that they were strongly opposed to Bolingbroke's proposed repeal of the Septennial Act. After the elections of that year, Pulteney and many of the Whigs began to hope that before long, either by making terms with Walpole or by overthrowing him, they would find themselves in office. In view of such a contingency, it would be well not to be trammelled with an alliance with Bolingbroke and the Tories, or indeed with the Jacobites. Accordingly, they dropped the principles of Patriotism, and they broke off their connection with Bolingbroke.

"While the Minister was not hard pushed," Bolingbroke wrote in 1736, "nor the prospect of succeeding to him near, they appeared to have but one end, the reformation of the Government. The destruction of the Minister was pursued only as a preliminary, but of essential and indispensable necessity to that end. But, when his destruction seemed to approach, the object of his succession interposed to the sight of many, and the reformation of the Government was no longer their point of view."

Various reasons combined to make Bolingbroke's retirement to France advisable. It was probable that Walpole's attack on him, during the debate, in 1734, on the repeal of the Septennial Act, might lead to something more serious. His own expenditure at Dawley had been very great, and pecuniary difficulties rendered economy necessary. Pulteney and his followers had thought that his "name and presence in England did hurt." Symptoms of a schism, too, in the Opposition were becoming visible; and it was apparent that Pulteney was now considering the best means of turning Walpole out without demanding any change in his system. He would thus, (as, indeed, happened), in Bolingbroke's words, merely substitute one faction for another. In a letter to Marchmont in 1746, Bolingbroke said: "I did not leave England in '35 till some schemes that were then on the loom, though they never came into effect, made me one too many, even for my intimate friends." Prudence, economy, and dignity combined to bring about his Second Exile.

During the ten years preceding 1735, his life in London and at Dawley was calculated to add enormously to his reputation as a Statesman and man of Letters. His organization of the heterogeneous sections in one workable Opposition, his writings in *The Craftsman*, *The Dissertation on Parties*, and those three bitter invectives against Walpole, known as *The Occasional Writer*, rendered the history of the struggle peculiarly interesting. At Dawley he became the centre of a group of writers, who were largely influenced by his brilliant conversation. All this was now over, and Dawley was put up for sale. In France, Bolingbroke divided his time between his favourite residence at Chanteloup, in Touraine, and his hunting-lodge at Argeville. Here he wrote his letter *On the True Use of Retirement and Study*, his letter *On the Spirit of Patriotism*, and began his letters *On the Study of History*.

The first of these was addressed to Lord Bathurst and is a short philosophical treatise after the manner of Seneca, in which he lays down that each person should be guided solely by his own reason. In this letter we see clearly the existence of the sceptical spirit with which he became later so thoroughly imbued.

The Letters on History, eight in number, were written for the benefit of Lord Cornbury, and were begun in November, 1735. The first five letters advocate the philosophical study of history, the object of which is, he declares, to improve men in virtue and wisdom, and to make them better men and better citizens. The credibility of early Greek history, of Jewish history, and of Scriptural chronology is the subject of a spirited attack, which is followed by eloquent and interesting observations on the advantages of historical study. In the last three letters is contained a sketch of European history from the beginning of the sixteenth century to the death of Anne, and an elaborate defence of his own conduct in making the Treaty of Utrecht. In spite of many inaccuracies, these letters bear remarkable testimony to his mental activity and to his power of memory, being written without books and with the aid of a few notes only. Pope, on reading them, wrote to Swift (March 25, 1736): "I have lately seen some writings of Lord B's since he went to France. Nothing can depress his genius; whatever befalls him, he will still be the greatest man in the world, either in his own time, or with posterity."

His essay on the *Spirit of Patriotism*, written in 1736, shortly after his departure from England, is instinct with rage and indignation at the failure of his own efforts, at the power of the governing faction, at the low aims and aspirations of a large portion of the people, at the conduct of the Malcontent Whigs, and finally at the inactivity of many of the Tories. The language throughout this very fine essay is striking. He attacks Walpole with bitter directness :—

"There have been monsters in other ages, and other countries, as well as ours. We will suppose a man impudent, rash, presumptuous, ungracious, insolent, and profligate, in speculation as well as practice. He can bribe, but he cannot seduce; he can buy, but he cannot gain; he can lie, but he cannot deceive."

He then points out that Walpole's strength was derived partly from corruption, partly from the steady policy of the Whigs to enrich themselves while impoverishing the rest of the nation, and :—

"by these and other means of establishing their dominion under the Government, and with the favour of a family who were foreigners, and therefore might believe that they were established on the throne by the goodwill and strength of this party alone."

The Malcontent Whigs, the followers of Pulteney, receive no mercy at his hands. Their patriotism was simulated, their desire for liberty a pretence, they embraced it faintly, they pursued it listlessly, "they are tired of it when they

have much to hope, and give it up when they have nothing
to fear." The members of his own party did not escape;
he accuses them of continuing sour, sullen, and inactive.

"They waited," he says, "like the Jews, for a Messiah that may never
come. . . . While they waited, they were marked out like the Jews, a
distinct race, hewers of wood and drawers of water, scarce members of the
community, though born in the country."

He expresses great surprise that, after the excitement
connected with the Excise Scheme, the elections had not
gone against the Government. In Parliament the opponents
of the Scheme were, he says strenuously supported for a
time, but the indolence and inactivity of the members of
the Opposition was such that all the excitement calmed
down before the elections. Parliament itself, he continues,
has engrossed all the executive power, and the nation sub-
mits to a tyranny which it would never suffer from a king.
Bolingbroke despairs of the present generation. There are
some good men among them, but:—

"they have been clogged, or misled, or overborne by others; and, seduced
by natural temper and inactivity, have taken to any excuse or yielded to
any pretence that favoured it."

He consoles himself with the thoughts that the new
generation which is coming on the stage will show more
spirit and virtue, and that "we must want spirit as well as
virtue to perish." We must not, however, be led to suppose
that Bolingbroke's despair continued to depress him for any
length of time. In June, 1738, he returned to England,
where events had occurred which seemed likely to have important results. Queen Caroline was dead, and she had
been one of Walpole's strongest supporters. The health of
George II. was precarious; a series of bad seasons, together
with a growing impatience at the peace policy of the
Government had shaken Walpole's popularity. Pulteney
and Carteret held aloof from Bolingbroke. They wished to
purify and strengthen the Whig party, while Shippen and

the Jacobites refused to give up the old-fashioned Toryism.
Neither Pulteney's Whig followers nor the ordinary Tory
country gentlemen would believe that party distinctions had
ceased ; only the Tories, under Wyndham and the " Boy
Patriots " in whose ranks were to be found Pitt and Lyttelton, Chesterfield, and Polwarth, Cobham, and Grenville,
still believed in Bolingbroke's doctrines.

A centre was found for those who desired the abolition
of party distinctions at Norfolk House in the person of
Frederick, Prince of Wales. Round him gathered all
Bolingbroke's followers. Frederick had already been struck
by Bolingbroke's conversational powers. In order to establish himself still further in the favour of the Prince, whom
he now regarded as the hope of the Opposition, and to
detach him from the influence of those Whigs who followed
Pulteney and Carteret, Bolingbroke wrote his *Idea of a Patriot
King*. Before he again left England, in the spring of 1739,
he had done much to pave the way for success in the future.
The affair of Jenkins' ear had roused the nation, which was
now clamouring for war. It was evident that Walpole's
fall was not far distant. To Bolingbroke the times were of
the profoundest interest ; his hopes seemed likely to be followed by the accession of " a coalition of parties meeting on
a national bottom." Though in France, he kept up close
relations with the Opposition. In 1739, in consequence of
the Convention of the Pardo with Spain, the Secession from
the House of Commons took place, rendered famous on
account of the eloquence of Wyndham's farewell speech,
written, it was said, by Bolingbroke. That statesman, however, had disapproved of the Secession in the first instance,
as Walpole was left at liberty to pursue his own measures.
Secessions have never been successful in English history.
Public opinion declared as strongly against this as it did
against the Whig Secession during the American struggle
for Independence. On October the 4th, 1739, war was de-

clared against Spain, and the Opposition again appeared in their places.

In 1740, the death of Sir William Wyndham, the skilful leader of the Tories, was a great blow to the Opposition, from which, in fact, it did not recover during Bolingbroke's life. "He was," as Lyttelton said in a letter to Bolingbroke, "the centre of union of the best men of all parties." As long as he was in Parliament, he was able to keep the Tories and Malcontent Whigs in some sort of order. Ever since 1735, there had been daily increasing signs that the Coalition was about to break up. Wyndham's presence alone prevented the carelessness, inactivity, and languor of the great part of the Opposition from ruining the attempts that were being made to effect a reformation of the Government. Lyttelton thought that, if the Prince of Wales could keep the Hanoverian Tories united under him with the uncorrupt part of the Whigs, the Coalition might be saved from impending destruction, and its objects steadily, regularly, and warmly pursued. To expect that Frederick, Prince of Wales, could play any such part was of course out of the question. And the disastrous effect of the death of Wyndham was at once seen. In the very moment of victory, the various sections of that Coalition, which had been formed with such labour by Bolingbroke, showed signs of revolt. The schism among the Malcontent Whigs, in 1735, had filled him with despair; the conduct of the Tory and Jacobite sections, in 1741, elicited from him a burst of indignation. On February the 13th, Sandys had moved in an address to the King the dismissal of Walpole. Some of the Tories voted against the motion, and among them was Bolingbroke's friend, Lord Cornbury; some did not vote at all, and with them was Shippen, with thirty-four Jacobites. "The conduct of the Tories," wrote Bolingbroke to Marchmont, "is silly, infamous, and void of any colour of excuse." He was particularly angry with the honest, incorruptible

Shippen, who seems to have disliked the Coalition against Walpole, to whom he was under an obligation. Bolingbroke goes on to regret the death of Wyndham :—

"He did not expect any more than I have long done to render this generation of Tories of much good use to this country. . . . But still, if he had lived, he would have hindered these stranger creatures—I can hardly call them men—from doing all the mischief they have lately done, and will, perhaps, continue to do."

The failure of the different sections of the Opposition to act together thus gave Walpole one more year of power, and made it evident to Bolingbroke that his grand idea of a fusion between the Malcontent Whigs, the Tories, and the Jacobites into one 'national party' in opposition to 'the gang' was impossible.

In February, 1742, Walpole fell, and in April, Bolingbroke's father, the old Lord St. John, died. On Bolingbroke's arrival in London from France, he found that all his hopes of a Coalition Ministry were dashed to the ground. The spirit of exclusiveness and selfishness lay heavy on the Whigs, and Pulteney and Carteret, acting as Bolingbroke had foreseen, completely threw over their Tory allies, and made a compromise with the subordinate members of Walpole's Ministry.

"I am sorry," Bolingbroke had written to Marchmont on April 6th, 1742, "to find that the forebodings of my mind are likely to be verified. I apprehend all that I see happen. How could I not? Long before I left Britain it was plain that some persons meant that the Opposition should serve as their scaffolding, nothing else ; and whenever they had a glimpse of hope that they might rise to power without it, they showed the greatest readiness to demolish it. Nothing, therefore, has happened which was not foreseen."

He might have watched events with more equanimity had he been able to dip into the future, and see how Pulteney's triumph was to be followed almost immediately by the collapse of his influence.

CHAPTER VII

BOLINGBROKE'S LATER YEARS.

1742–1751.

In August, 1742, Bolingbroke returned to Argeville, having had a narrow escape of capture by three Spanish privateers at anchor near Calais. In order to pursue his studies, free from interruption, he had fitted a small pavilion in the garden of the abbey of Sens. It was at this time that he wrote many of the works for which he is so famous.

At the beginning of 1743, he was again in England, and stayed partly at his house at Battersea, then inhabited by Lord Marchmont, partly with Pope at Twickenham. He threw himself with all his old keenness into the plans of the Opposition. Lord Wilmington was nominally Prime Minister, but Carteret was virtually head of the Government. On questions of home and foreign policy, Carteret and Bolingbroke were diametrically opposed. Carteret had always, even when leading the Opposition to Walpole in the House of Lords, confessed to Bolingbroke that he intended to carry on the old system, though Bolingbroke afterwards bitterly complained of his having abandoned, when in office, the principles he held when in Opposition.

"The principles of the late Opposition," he had written to Polwarth, "were the principles of very few of the opposers; and your Lordship and I, and some few, very few besides, were the bubbles of men whose advantage lies in having worse hearts; for I am not humble enough to allow them better heads."

Carteret's foreign policy was designated by Bolingbroke as madness. Our war with Spain had broken out in 1739. The Emperor, Charles VI., died in 1740, and the invasion of Silesia took place, followed by the invasion of the Austrian dominions by the French, in the interests of Bavaria. Carteret's policy was to reconcile Frederick the Great and Maria Theresa, to withdraw the Elector of Bavaria (the Emperor, Charles VII.) from the French alliance, and to secure the co-operation of the Dutch. In other words, he wished to form a united Germany, capable of resisting French aggression, by means of a revival of the Grand Alliance.

Bolingbroke had always allowed that, at the Peace of 1713, France was left too powerful. Though Carteret's policy was in a manner to complete the work left unfinished at Utrecht, the Tories had always consistently opposed the system of Continental alliances, and Bolingbroke had ever entertained feelings of hostility to the Hapsburgs. It was natural that he should look with great aversion on a scheme of policy which would lead to the extension of the Hapsburg ascendancy.

He was now anxious, if possible, to form a coalition of the Pelhams and the Tories against Carteret. But the principal supporters of his views had been removed from the House of Commons. Wyndham had died in 1740; Polwarth had, on the death of his father, become the third Earl of Marchmont, and, not being an elected Scottish Peer, had no seat in the House of Lords.

"What a star has our Minister," Bolingbroke had written at the time, "Wyndham dead, Marchmont disabled! the loss of Marchmont and Wyndham to our country." In June, 1743, he left England, and returned to France.

After a month at Argeville, where he heard the news of the battle of Dettingen, won by his old friend Lord Stair, he was ordered by his physicians to spend the month of September at Aix-la-Chapelle on account of his gout and rheumatism. From Aix-la-Chapelle he corresponded frequently with Marchmont on the political outlook in England. In October he returned to England, partly to place his private affairs on a more satisfactory footing, partly to try and bring about a coalition. Wilmington had died in July, and Henry Pelham had become Prime Minister. There was little chance of putting the scheme of a coalition into execution, and Bolingbroke spent the remainder of 1743 and the early part of 1744 at Battersea with his friend Marchmont. Once again, in June, 1744, he crossed the Channel, but owing to the critical outlook on the Continent, he speedily returned, and settled for the remainder of his life in the old Manor House at Battersea. There he and Lady Bolingbroke received many of the rising young politicians, who were delighted to listen to the conversation of the statesman who had negotiated the Peace of Utrecht. Thither came, in addition to Marchmont and old Lord Stair, Lyttelton, Secretary to the Prince of Wales, Chesterfield, Murray, the Solicitor-General, and William Pitt.

The political situation in the autumn of 1744 was full of interest to Bolingbroke and his friends the "Boy Patriots," who had hitherto coalesced with no party. In June, 1744, the relations between Carteret an l the Pelhams had become very strained. A crisis was evidently at hand, and the possibility of a Coalition Government was ever in Bolingbroke's mind. It was not, however, till November that Carteret's removal from office was demanded by the Pelhams.

In spite of his vigorous intellect, his knowledge of European politics, his steady purpose and his patriotism, Carteret (since October, 1744, Lord Granville) was driven from active political life by the great Revolution families, who had by this time firmly riveted their yoke on the Crown. The selfish and bureaucratic Whigs had trampled over the more independent section of the party represented by Carteret. One result of the struggle was the reconstitution of the Ministry, and what was known as the " Broad Bottom Administration " was formed, which included many of Bolingbroke's friends like Chesterfield. During 1745 the Pelhams carried on the war with little success, while at home they were regarded by the King with displeasure. In the autumn of the year, in order to strengthen themselves, they proposed to George that Pitt, who was exceedingly distasteful to him, should be made Secretary-at-War. The King's refusal was followed by the resignation of the Foreign Secretaries, Newcastle and Harrington, in February, 1746, in the midst of the Jacobite rebellion. Then took place what is known as the Three Days Revolution. George placed the Foreign Department in the hands of Granville, and made Pulteney, now Lord Bath, First Lord of the Treasury. They were not supported by any Tories, nor did they receive any sympathy in either House of Parliament. The remaining Ministers resigned, and George was forced to yield. The victory of the Pelhams was complete, and the Whig oligarchy ruled supreme till the accession of George III. Bolingbroke himself had the supreme satisfaction of seeing the failure of both Bath and Granville, the former being First Lord for one day, the latter Secretary of State for less than four days.

He had regarded the Jacobite movement of '45 with indifference, and advised Marchmont to do the same. Like the majority of the nation, he did not interest himself in the slightest degree in the cause of Charles Edward or of George II.

"I expect," he wrote to Marchmont, "no good news, and I am therefore contented to have none. I wait with much resignation to know to what lion's paw we are to fall."

His life, however, was drawing to a close, and old age, as it crept on, brought with it the sad experiences which are the lot of those who live long. In May, 1744, he had stood by the deathbed of Pope; in October, 1745, the unhappy Swift breathed his last in Ireland. Visitors ceased to come as frequently as in former days, and Bolingbroke felt keenly their absence. He was especially angry at not being treated by Pitt with more deference. In July, 1746, he wrote to Marchmont:—

"It is time I should retire for good and all from the world, and from the very approaches to business, *ne peccem*. I put it into prose, ' *ad extremum ridendus*.' If I have showed too much zeal—for I own that this even in a good cause may be pushed into some degree of ridicule—I can show as much indifference ; and surely it is time for me to show the latter, since I am come to the even of a tempestuous day, and see in the whole extent of our horizon no signs that to-morrow will be fairer."

In spite of these assertions, he continued till his death to watch with interest the war on the Continent. The Peace of Aix-la-Chapelle, concluded in 1748, drew from him *Some Reflections on the Present State of the Nation.* Though unfinished, the *Reflections* are important as containing what were probably his real views on the course of our foreign policy from the accession of Anne. In them is seen clearly his animosity towards the Hapsburgs. He declares that in both the Spanish and Austrian Succession Wars the Court of Vienna sacrificed nothing, but that our sacrifices were enormous. Maria Theresa, he says—

"seemed to make war just as it suited her convenience, to save all the expense she could in the Netherlands, to plunder all she could in Italy, and to make us pay the whole immense subsidies which we gave her for both."

After having blamed the part taken by England in "this strange war," he draws an alarming picture of England's condition, comparing it to the state of France under Henry IV., at the time of the Peace of Vervins:—

"Are we not as near to bankruptcy as the French nation was at that time, and much more so than they are at this time? May not confusion follow it here as well as there? And, finally, may not the joint ambition of two branches of Bourbon in some future conjunction produce effects as fatal, and much more, to us, if we continue in our present state of impotence till such a conjuncture happens, as was to be feared by France at the time we speak of from the joint ambition of two branches of Austria?"

The load of debt under which England then laboured caused him much concern, and he feared that, "if we do not pay our debts, we must sink under them." Though he allows that trade gives us wealth, he cannot bring himself to regard the merchant class with favour: "the landed men are the true owners of our political vessels; the moneyed men as such are no more than passengers." The gloomy views he took of the condition of England sound curiously to those who remember that some twelve years later, under the influence of Pitt, victories, which recalled the triumphs of Marlborough, resulted in the foundation of the British Empire.

In the same year, under the editorship of David Mallet, the Under-Secretary to the Prince of Wales, and described by Dr. Johnson as the only native of Scotland of whom Scotchmen were not proud, Bolingbroke gave to the world a volume containing the *Spirit of Patriotism, the Idea of a Patriot King*, and the *Account of the State of Parties at the Accession of George I*. In the preface appeared a violent attack on Pope for having secretly had fifteen hundred copies of the *Patriot King* printed from the manuscript lent him by Bolingbroke, with the result that a portion of that essay had already appeared in the pages of a magazine. Pope's old literary ally, Warburton, defended with spirit the memory of his dead friend. The public declared unmistakably for Warburton. Pope had certainly acted badly, but he had been dead five years, and had written warmly in praise of Bolingbroke in the *Essay on Man*. Bolingbroke found that, as Chesterfield told him, he had succeeded in uniting against himself Whigs, Tories, Trimmers, and Jacobites. Mr. Stebbing, however, in his Essay on *Henry St. John*, thinks that Bolingbroke's rage is to be attributed rather to Pope's choice of Warburton as his literary executor, than to his discovery of Pope's breach of faith.

On March the 18th, 1751, Lady Bolingbroke died, after a long illness. To Bolingbroke the loss of his wife, to whom he was greatly attached and whose companionship had been a solace to him in his ever-increasing infirmities, was very severe. She had mingled in the society of Louis XIV.'s court, and seems to have been a very pleasant, intelligent Frenchwoman, with all the grace and *savoir faire* of the Faubourg St. Germain. On her death her relatives disputed the validity of her marriage, and claimed her property. After a long lawsuit the Parliament of Paris reversed the decision of the Lower Court, which had been given in favour of the relatives. All Paris was delighted at the result, and the President of the Grande Chambre expressed sentiments of admiration for the late distinguished statesman; for Bolingbroke had died a few weeks before the decision.

In the autumn of 1750 he had made his will. In August, 1751, he wrote from Battersea to his half-sister, Lady Luxborough, to urge her to come to him, as he was too ill to leave his home, and offering to send a coach and horses to bring her to him. Unfortunately, Lady Luxborough was herself " a prisoner in the sick-room at the time." Early in December, 1751, he became convinced his end was near, and took leave of Chesterfield with the words :—" God, who placed me here, will do what He pleases with me hereafter; and He knows best what to do. May He bless you." A few days later, on December the 12th, after a short period of severe suffering, overcome with the consciousness of continued failure ever since the conclusion of the Peace of Utrecht, but instinct to the last with energy, Henry St. John, a man endowed with the most varied and glorious gifts, passed away. Six days later he was buried in the same vault as his second wife in Battersea Church.

The St. Johns were a long-lived race. Sir Walter had died at the ripe age of eighty-seven; Lord St. John lived till he was over ninety, and Bolingbroke had, when he died, passed his seventy-third birthday. Born during the reign of Charles II., a Member of Parliament in the reign of William III., and living into the second half of the eighteenth century, it may well be said of him that "he seems to link together the twilight age of the Stuarts and the grey dawn of visibly modern times."

CHAPTER VIII

REVIEW OF BOLINGBROKE'S CAREER AND CHARACTER.

Always struggling against an adverse fate—The death of Anne—The fall of Walpole—His failure to secure the reversal of his attainder—His transcendent abilities—His writings—Illustrations—His correspondence—Eloquence—His general intellectual qualities—His power of application—Views taken by Mr. Lecky and Mr. Harrop of his character—His faults—The child of his age—His enormous personal influence—Love of hunting—His horses and dogs—His life at Bucklersbury, Ashdown Park, La Source, Dawley, Chanteloup—The last years of his life at Battersea—His influence over young statesmen—His European position.

THERE is something inexpressibly sad in contemplating Bolingbroke's career. It would appear as though he was always struggling against an adverse fate. All through his life he was busy conceiving and attempting to carry out the most brilliant *tours de force*; and just when he seemed on the verge of success, at the very moment of triumph, his schemes, like a house built with a pack of cards, were dashed to the ground, and the whole work of reconstruction had to be recommenced. On two celebrated occasions, when the cup of victory was at his lips, Fortune had interposed and condemned him, like Tantalus, to forbear. In 1714 he had only wanted six weeks more, six short weeks, in order to place the Tory party on a firm foundation, from which it would have commanded the whole position and dictated its own terms. All the struggles, the diplomacy, the risks, the fears of those fateful four years had been faced with one end in view. He had, like a traveller on a dark night in a strange country, fixed his eyes on a distant light, and had made up his mind that his safety lay in reaching that light, no matter what obstacles crossed his path. A war, the objects of which had been popular, was raging; negotiations for peace were at once set on foot. Unless, however, the mercantile class was satisfied, the blood of the Ministers would be demanded; terms were forced from Louis which satisfied the whole trading interest. At home the Tories were furious at the absence of attacks on the Nonconformists; Bolingbroke gave them the Schism Act. Oxford wavered and vacillated; Bolingbroke seized the leadership of the party some months before the Prime Minister resigned. We know the result.

Again, when after his return from exile he threw himself into the struggle against Walpole, with what hopes did he enter on the campaign! Towards the end of George I.'s reign he had his well-known interview with the King, and Walpole's fall seemed a not impossible event. But the King died soon afterwards, and the accession of George II. offered no hopes to the fallen Statesman of a return to office. He therefore redoubled his attacks upon Walpole. The difficulties in the way of forming a powerful Opposition to the Minister appeared insuperable, but he overcame them. The Jacobites and the Whigs agreed apparently to sink their differences, and to ignore the fact that their principles were diametrically opposed. With infinite labour, extending over some nine years, he had welded together, out of the heterogeneous atoms of Whigs, Tories, Jacobites, and literary men, a well-compacted Opposition, united in fierce hostility to the great Whig Minister. In 1733 the hitherto impregnable position seemed likely to be taken by storm, and in 1734 the hopes of the assailants were high. The next year Bolingbroke was in France trying to find in his books consolation for the baseness of his allies. But his efforts had not been in vain. He had shattered the wall, and in 1742 his former friends and allies entered into the city and enjoyed the fruits of his now famous exertions. The friendship of the Whigs was more fatal to the Tories in the eighteenth century than their hostility. *Timeo Danaos et dona ferentes* might well have been on Bolingbroke's lips in 1742.

And, if the life of Bolingbroke be examined more closely, disappointment will be seen ever dogging his steps. He hoped, by means of an interview with George I., to effect the fall of Walpole. He had the interview, and though it had no immediate result there is no doubt that as long as George I. lived Bolingbroke's hopes of a complete restoration were not unfounded.

The death of George I., however, like the death of Queen Anne was a fatal blow to Bolingbroke's expectations. The accession of George II. brought with it no realization of the hopes of the Opposition. In his private aims, too, Bolingbroke encountered failure. He was till the day of his death bent on reviving in himself the Earldom granted to a member of the family by James I., and which had become extinct in 1711. On finding that only the lower step in the Peerage had been given him in 1712 he wrote to Strafford in great anger. " I own to you that I felt more indignation than ever I had done." He continued throughout his life to pursue the visionary Earldom, and expected to receive it when Frederick, Prince of Wales, became King. But Frederick died in March, 1751, and Bolingbroke never secured the Earldom.

If it be remembered that most of his days were spent in Opposition, the loss to the nation seems immense. One feels that the times were indeed " out of joint " when, by a series of accidents and by a system of party Government, England was deprived during the greater part of his life of the services of one of her ablest sons. And of his transcendent ability there is no question. His " genius and daring," Mr. Lecky writes, " were incontestable." In brilliancy and impetuosity he had no equal. His style, though at times diffuse and declamatory, is usually brilliant and spirited.

Chesterfield declared that until he had read the *Letters on Patriotism* and *The Patriot King*, he "did not know all the extent and powers of the English language." No more striking passages in his works can be found than his famous dissertation on eloquence and his delineation of Demosthenes and Cicero in the pages of the essay on the *Spirit of Patriotism*. The following extracts will probably be read with interest :—

"Eloquence has charms to lead mankind, and gives a nobler superiority than power, that every dunce may use, or fraud, that every knave may employ. But eloquence must flow, like a stream that is fed by an abundant spring, and not spout forth a little frothy water on some gaudy day, and remain dry the rest of the year. The famous orators of Greece and Rome were the statesmen and ministers of those commonwealths. The nature of their governments, and the humour of those ages, made elaborate orations necessary. They harangued oftener than they debated ; and the *ars dicendi* required more study and more exercise of mind and of body too, among them, than are necessary among us. But, as much pains as they took in learning how to conduct the stream of eloquence, they took more to enlarge the fountain from which it flowed. Hear Demosthenes, hear Cicero thunder against Philip, Catiline, and Antony. I choose the example of the first rather than that of Pericles, whom he imitated, or of Phocion, whom he opposed, or of any other considerable personage in Greece ; and the example of Cicero rather than that of Crassus, or of Hortensius, or of any other of the great men of Rome, because the eloquence of these two has been so celebrated, that we are accustomed to look upon them almost as mere orators. They were orators indeed, and no man who has a soul can read their orations, after the revolution of so many ages, after the extinction of the governments, and of the people for whom they were composed, without feeling, at this hour, the passions they were designed to move, and the spirit they were designed to raise" (*Works*, vol. iv., pp. 214, 215).

The latter part of his description of the secret of Cicero's oratorical success is particularly striking :—

"His eloquence in private causes gave him first credit at Rome ; but it was this knowledge, this experience, and the continued habits of business that supported his reputation, enabled him to do so much service to his country, and gave force and authority to his eloquence. To little purpose would he have attacked Catiline with all the vehemence that indignation, and even fear, added to eloquence, if he had trusted to this weapon alone.

This weapon alone would have secured neither him nor the Senate from the poniard of that assassin. He would have had no occasion to boast that he had driven this infamous citizen out of the walls of Rome, 'abiit, excessit, evasit, erupit,' if he had not made it beforehand impossible for him to continue any longer in them. As little occasion would he have had to assume the honour of defeating, without any tumult or any disorder, the designs of those who conspired to murder the Roman people, to destroy the Roman empire, and to extinguish the Roman name ; if he had not united, by skill and management in the common cause of their country, orders of men the most averse to each other, if he had not watched all the machinations of the conspirators in silence, and prepared a strength sufficient to resist them, at Rome and in the provinces, before he opened this scene of villainy to the Senate and the people. In a word, if he had not made much more use of political prudence, that is, of the knowledge of mankind, and of the arts of government, which study and experience give, than of all the powers of his eloquence" (vol. iv., pp. 218, 219).

His correspondence with his intimate friends, such as Pope and Swift, is as a rule delightful, though often marred by an affectation of distaste for the world. His *Political Correspondence* contains the letters of a man of business. They go straight to the point, and are admirably clear and precise.

"Were Lord Bolingbroke to write to an emperor or to a statesman," Pope remarked, "he would fix on that point which was the most material, would place it in the strongest and finest light, and manage it so as to make it most serviceable for his purpose."

In wit and eloquence he is far superior to any of his contemporaries. Of his conversational powers Chesterfield speaks highly :—

"His manner of speaking in private conversation is just as elegant as his writings. Whatever subject he either speaks or writes upon, he adorns it with the most splendid eloquence ; not a studied or laboured eloquence, but such a flowing happiness of diction, which (from care, perhaps, at first) is become so habitual to him, that even his most familiar conversations, if taken down in writing, would bear the press, without the least correction, either as to method or to style."

And the same writer's testimony to his eloquence is interesting as coming from a hostile witness :—

"I am old enough to have heard him speak in Parliament, and I remember that, though prejudiced against him by party, I felt all the force and charms of his eloquence. Like Belial in Milton,

'He made the worst appear the better cause.'

All the internal and external advantages and talents of an orator are undoubtedly his; figure, voice, elocution, knowledge, and, above all, the purest and most florid diction, with the justest metaphors and happiest images, had raised him to the post of Secretary-at-War, at four-and-twenty years old."

Lord Brougham's opinion was that "if Bolingbroke spoke as he wrote, he must have been the greatest of modern orators, as far as composition goes."

Though, unfortunately, owing to the imperfections of the *Parliamentary History* for Queen Anne's reign, none of his speeches have come down to us, we can get some idea of his eloquence from the following passage from the *Dissertation of Parties* :

"If King Charles had found the nation plunged in corruption, the people choosing their representatives for money, without any other regard, and these representatives of the people, as well as the nobility, reduced by luxury to beg the unhallowed alms of a Court, or to receive, like miserable hirelings, the wages of iniquity from a minister—if he had found the nation, I say, in this condition (which extravagant supposition one cannot make without horror), he might have dishonoured her abroad, and impoverished and oppressed her at home, though he had been the weakest prince on earth, and his Ministers the most odious and contemptible men that ever presumed to be ambitious. Our fathers might have fallen into circumstances which compose the very quintessence of political misery. They might have sold their 'birthright for porridge,' which was their own ; they might have been bubbled by the foolish, bullied by the fearful, and insulted by those whom they despised. They would have deserved to be slaves, and they might have been treated as such. When a free people crouch like camels to be loaded, the next at hand, no matter who, mounts them, and they soon feel the whip and the spur of their tyrant ; for a tyrant, whether prince or minister, resembles the devil in many respects, particularly in this, he is often both the tempter and tormentor. He makes the criminal, and he punishes the crime" (vol. iii., pp. 110, 111).

This passage, which was much admired by Lord Brougham, well carries out what Bolingbroke himself once said, that " eloquence must flow like a stream that is fed by an abundant spring," and inclines me to believe that he dictated most of his writings to an amanuensis.

The whole of the eighth Letter on *The Study of History*, which contains his defence of the Treaty of Utrecht, is nothing less than a brilliant speech. Brougham relates of Pitt that,

" when the conversation rolled upon lost works, and some said they should prefer restoring the books of Livy, some of Tacitus, and some a Latin tragedy, he at once decided for a speech of Bolingbroke."

In this eighth Letter Pitt might have found a masterpiece of Parliamentary oratory unsurpassed in Bolingbroke's age. It was undoubtedly his eloquence which brought him into the foremost ranks of the Tory party and secured his rapid advance. It is always said that Walpole's fear of the influence of his oratory in the House of Lords was the principal reason of his refusal to allow Bolingbroke to re-enter Parliamentary life. There is no doubt whatever that Henry St. John was the first orator of his age. His intellectual qualities were of a high order, he had an intimate acquaintance with the great authors of antiquity, he had a perfect mastery of French and Italian, and a fair acquaintance with Spanish. He loved learning and litera-ture for its own sake ; he excelled in history ; he explored " the unknown and unknowable regions of metaphysics." As he had a great love of acquiring knowledge and a mar-vellously retentive memory, it is no surprise to read that " the relative political and commercial interests of every country in Europe, particularly of his own, are better known to him than perhaps to any man in it." His clear conception of the exigencies of a situation and of the neces-sary means to be adopted, his power of seizing opportunities, and the possession of the valuable instinct of leading men, marks him out as a true statesman.

Nor can it be objected that in him the more solid qualities which in such an eminent degree distinguished his rival, Robert Walpole, causing sober people to regard the Norfolk squire with something akin to enthusiasm, were wanting in Bolingbroke. His application astounded all who knew him. " He engaged young," wrote Chesterfield, " and distinguished himself in business, and his penetration was almost intuition." " He would plod," according to Swift, " whole days and nights like the lowest clerk in an office." Marlborough and Godolphin were delighted with the diligence of the young Secretary-at-War, who had applied himself with such energy to master the intricate financial and military details of his office. The history of England's statesmen furnishes few examples of such capacity and ability, combined with such power of application and concentration, as were to be found united in the person of Bolingbroke.

In spite of these very remarkable powers, he was, owing to the political circumstances of his day, only in office from 1704 to 1708, and from 1710 to 1714, and of those eight years his only opportunity of showing his real statesmanlike qualities was during the last four years of Anne's reign. Before 1704 he was on the side of the Government, and busy in making his way. From 1715 to 1751, when his powers were at their best, he was in perpetual Opposition, employing his energies, so well adapted to political life, either in the service of a faction or in writing brilliant but, generally speaking, ephemeral essays. This exclusion from a Parliamentary career during these thirty-six years was due to his flight, the great mistake of his life. It is impossible to guess to what extent his continued presence in Parliament would have modified the Whig triumph. Would he ever have gained, or, if gained, continued to enjoy, the unanimous confidence of the Tory party? Mr. Lecky would reply in the negative.

" His eminently Italian character," he writes, " delighting in elaborate intrigue, the contrast between his private life and his stoical professions, his notorious indifference to the religious tenets which were the very basis of the politics of his party, shook the confidence of the country gentry and country clergy, who formed the bulk of his followers" (*History of England in the Eighteenth Century*, vol. i., p. 131).

Mr. Harrop, in his *Political Study and Criticism of Boling-broke* (pp. 191, 192), takes the same view in more elaborate language :

" His polished manners, his lively wit, his quick perceptions, his facile speech, his ready invention, the ease with which he caught and mimicked the intemperate tone of his rude supporters, his fondness for subterfuge and artifice, his affection of philosophical indifference to the objects for which he was at the moment most eagerly striving, his vanity, his industry, his simulated idleness, his unfeigned respect for speculative truth, the vastness and boldness of his political enterprises, the nervous apprehension of physical danger, the loftiness of his moral conceptions . . . all these things were the marks of a character which, in its strange and various traits, an Italian of the great age of Florence would have studied with respectful interest, but which repelled the Trullibers and Westerns from its very dis-similarity to their own."

His faults were partly hereditary, partly due to the manners of the time. " Violent partisanship," it has been said, ran in his blood. In the Barons' War, in the struggle of Henry VII. against Pretenders to his throne, in the Irish wars of Elizabeth, members of the St. John family were to be found. In the seventeenth century the combative and partisan nature of the family still more strongly asserted itself, various members of the different branches into which the family was divided fighting respectively for King and Parliament. And Bolingbroke found in the politics of his day ample opportunity for the exercise of his partisan spirit. During the whole of Anne's reign, party considerations were mixed up inextricably with every question of home or foreign policy. The absence of political morality in the statesmen of the day needs no demonstration. Boling-broke's own mercurial temperament fell in too readily with the prevailing sentiments of his time. Circumstances made opportunism the characteristic of his age, and Bolingbroke, like Marlborough, Shrewsbury, Harley, and, in fact, like most of the leading politicians, tends at times, especially in the reign of George II., to lay himself open to the charge of opportunism.

" He has noble and generous sentiments," wrote Chesterfield, "rather than fixed reflected principles of good nature and friendship; but they are more violent than lasting, and suddenly and often varied to their opposite extremes, with regard even to the same persons."

Always impulsive and impetuous, "his virtues and his vices, his reason and his passions did not," Chesterfield tells us, " blend themselves by a gradation of tints, but formed a shining and sudden contrast." His conduct and actions, however intemperate at times, did not preclude the existence from his youth upwards of a devouring ambition, which pursued him all his life, and which seems to have not only deprived him of the power of appreciating the meaning of peace and content, but led him at times into violent courses. Mr. Wyon thinks that his ambition in 1715 had stifled his patriotism, and that, had he thought the project a feasible one, he would, for the sake of retention of office, have brought in the Pretender. This also seems to be the view held by Count Rémusat. To this insane thirst for power Mr. Wyon also attributes Bolingbroke's blunder in joining the Jacobites. To gain the support of his extreme Tory followers he allowed an intolerant Bill to pass, though he himself despised the men who persecuted their religious opponents. The opinion held by Torcy and the Scotch Jacobites that he was insincere was probably erroneous, due to their ignorance of the English Constitution. The Spanish Ministers in the early part of the seventeenth century fell into the same blunder. They thought James I. was all-powerful, and could restore Roman Catholicism by a wave of his hand; the French Minister similarly was unable to understand why Anne and her Ministers could not repeal the Act of Settlement and bring in James Edward. Throughout his life, Bolingbroke was always full of self-confidence, struggling to be first, in no matter what circumstances he found himself. He took the lead in literary coteries, and in social clubs, no less than in the Cabinet of a Ministry, and in the deliberations of the Opposition. His talents gave him the foremost position, and he always had a considerable number of devoted followers. His outbursts of recklessness and defects in judgment tended to modify his fitness to lead a large and influential party. His correspondence indeed goes to show that his individuality made itself felt on all with whom he came in contact. Walpole feared its power; Pulteney fell under its influence; the "Boy Patriots" all yielded to the fascination of the personality of the old statesman. In 1712 the dignity of his manners and his handsome presence had made a profound impression on the French nobility.

Want of consistency is to be found in much of his life and writings, due in great measure, to the peculiar circumstances of the times. As the history of the life of this remarkable man is studied, it will be seen that he is distinctly the child of an age full of inconsistencies and contradictions. The reign of Anne found the Church a powerful corporation in touch with the mass of the nation; Bolingbroke led the High Church party. The eighteenth century, before it has far advanced, shakes off its earlier religious enthusiasm, and becomes scientific, materialistic, the age of common sense; Bolingbroke, the friend of Voltaire, becomes the exponent of a crude rationalism.

His intense political interests did not preclude the existence of a genuine love of the country and country pursuits. Like his rival Walpole, he had keen sporting tastes. At Bucklersbury, at Ashdown Park, at La Source, Dawley, and at Argeville, he took the most genuine pleasure in his hounds and horses. His beautiful home at Bucklersbury lay in the heart of the country. There he had spent most of the two years of his first retirement from political life; during the last four years of Anne's reign he was very fond of driving there from Windsor and spending a night or two in the country. At Bucklersbury he was no longer the statesman, but the model country gentleman, interested in his garden and his hounds. He would smoke with his neighbours, and discuss the affairs of the country and the prospects of the crops. Swift describes how he went in the summer of 1711 to Bucklersbury, and how Mr. Secretary was a perfect country gentleman there. " He smoked tobacco with one or two neighbours, he inquired after the wheat in such a field, he went to visit his hounds, and knew all their names." A considerable part of these years he spent at Peterborough's house at Parson's Green, Fulham, which the erratic Earl had allowed him to use. Even in the autumn of 1713, Bolingbroke, in spite of the critical state of affairs, found time to combine with politics the enjoyment of his favourite pursuit. A letter to Strafford, dated Ashdown Park, October the 8th, begins : " Tired as I am with fox hunting, since the messenger is to return immediately to London, I cannot neglect," etc. We find also a letter to the Duc d'Aumont, the French Ambassador, dated, *De mon Ecurie le* 21*me Octobre,* 1713, and beginning : " Parmi les chiens et les chevaux, au milieu de la plus profonde retraite, je n'ai rien à souhaiter pour être tout-à-fait heureux que la conversation du cher Duc d'Aumont," etc. On December the 3rd of the same year, writing to Sir John Stanley, he excuses the delay of General Evans in setting out for his command on the plea that his Colonel, " young Hawley, had the misfortune to break his bones in fox hunting with me."

La Source, whither he retired in 1720, was a beautiful spot. There he, as usual, combined study and field sports, and took a great interest in beautifying his new home.

"I have in my wood," he wrote to Swift on July the 21st, 1721, "the biggest and clearest spring in Europe. . . . If in a year's time you should find leisure to write to me, send me some mottoes for groves, and streams, and fine prospects and retreats, and contempt for grandeur, etc. I have one for my green-houses, and one for an alley which leads to my apartment, which are happy enough. The first is, *Hic ver assiduum atque alienis mensibus æstas ;* the other is, *Fallentis semita vitæ.*"

At Dawley he built stables and kennels, and expended, it is said, £23,000 on improvements. During his first autumn there he was thrown from his horse : "I am in great concern," wrote Swift to Pope, "at what I am just told is in some of the newspapers, that Lord Bolingbroke is much hurt by a fall in hunting." Swift's fears proved, however, groundless, as Pope wrote, in answer, to assure him that "Lord Bolingbroke had not the least harm by his fall." On his retirement to France, in 1735, he divided his time between Chanteloup and his hunting-lodge at Arge-ville. At both residences he was surrounded by horses and dogs. It is difficult to understand why the editor of the latest edition of Pope's works should indulge in the sneer that Bolingbroke "at least thought himself attached to the diversion of hunting." The minute details into which he enters in his correspondence with Wyndham about his dogs and horses point to a real interest in these things, not to a mere attempt

> "To beguile the thing he was
> By seeming otherwise."

When he finally settled at Battersea, in 1744, his health was much broken. Pitt found him dogmatic and pedantic, often querulous and fretful. It is a matter of regret that Pitt only knew him when he was succumbing to the infirmities of age. He was much attached to his wife, and a good master to his servants, whom he remembered in his will. He was kind and good-natured in ordinary life. Mrs. Delaney, the niece of Sir John Stanley, remembered sitting when a child on Lord Bolingbroke's knee at a puppet-show. He always treated his half-brothers with great consideration. George, the eldest, had received from him constant assistance, and on his early death Bolingbroke helped the two younger brothers. At Battersea his household was mainly French. His position as Lord of the Manor brought with it performance of certain duties. We find him commissioning Marchmont to buy him "a decent Common Prayer Book, such an one as a Lord of the Manor may hold forth to the edification of the parish. Let it be quarto." At times, too, he occupied the family pew in the old parish church. As old age crept on he stayed more and more at home. In September, 1746, he visited Lord Cornbury in Oxfordshire, where he met, among others, Pitt, then Paymaster of the Forces. In 1747 his old enemies, gout and rheumatism, drove him to Bath. From that time he was constantly a cripple, and frequently deprived of the use of his right hand.

With his death England lost a statesman who in good and evil fortunes made his personality felt on all who came across his path. " The Opposition," wrote the late Mr. Leadam, " was sensibly weakened by the death of their inspirer, Bolingbroke." In both public and in private life he had always been the centre of a political party or of a literary coterie. At La Source, at Chanteloup, at Dawley, and at Battersea, we see him surrounded by an admiring throng of visitors, who were for the most part attracted by his marvellous conversational powers, and to whom he discoursed on philosophy and politics. His successful conclusion of the Peace of Utrecht, his share in the overthrow of Walpole, his influence not only on the rising English politicians, but also on Pope and on Voltaire, combined to raise him to an almost European position. In expressing his admiration of the deceased Statesman, in March, 1752, the President of the Grand Chamber of the Parliament of Paris only reflected the sentiment of all men who have studied the political aims and literary career of the Great Lord Bolingbroke.

CHAPTER IX

BOLINGBROKE'S LITERARY FRIENDSHIPS.

Close connection between politics and literature—Its results—Defoe—
Importance of political writings—Addison — John Philips—Boling-
broke's literary friends — Pope—Parnell — Arbuthnot—Prior—Gay—
Swift—Society of Brothers—Effect of Anne's death—Bolingbroke at
Dawley—Pope at Twickenham—Meeting of the survivors of the
Scriblerus Club—The correspondence of Bolingbroke, Pope, and Swift
—Influence of Bolingbroke on Pope—The *Essay on Man*—The *Moral
Essays—Satires and Epistles of Horace imitated*—Devotion of Pope to
Bolingbroke—Influence of Pope on Bolingbroke—Voltaire's relations
with Bolingbroke—They meet first at La Source—Voltaire's exile—
Comes to England—Studies English literature—Influence of Boling-
broke on Voltaire's *Lettres sur les Anglais*—Voltaire's philosophical
views—Extent of the influence of Bolingbroke's deistical opinions on
Voltaire—Bolingbroke's literary tastes and literary friendships.

OF the statesmen who are no longer with us there is no
name more intimately connected with literature than that of
Bolingbroke. His influence on the whole train of thought,
and consequently on the productions of two men as dis-
similar as were Pope and Voltaire, is most marked. A very
delightful volume might be written upon Bolingbroke as a
man of letters. In an age singularly fertile in prose writers,
who were remarkable for the elegance and lucidity of their
style, Bolingbroke more than held his own. In an age
distinguished for the exquisite skill in its versification,
Bolingbroke was considered competent to revise the proofs
of one of the most renowned poems of the greatest master
of style in the eighteenth century. In an age when epistolary correspondence was the fashion, Bolingbroke's letters
will bear comparison with the correspondence of Lady Mary
Montague or with the letters of Pope.

The patron of struggling authors, the friend and protector of Dryden, the intimate friend and companion of Pope, Voltaire, and Swift, an author of some of the most interesting political disquisitions ever written, Bolingbroke will be handed down to posterity as a distinguished member of that brotherhood of literary statesmen which includes such men as Burke and Canning, and in our own day has seen added to its ranks Lord Beaconsfield and Lord Morley, Lord Iddesleigh and Mr. Gladstone.

Though he may be said, like all lovers of books, to have read continuously, there are two periods in his life when his connection with literature and literary men is especially worthy of notice. In the first of these periods, which ended with his flight to France, he was the centre of that brilliant throng of men of letters who gave such a peculiar lustre to the reign of Queen Anne. A well-known characteristic of her reign, and to some extent of that of George I., was the close connection existing between politics and literature, a connection which brought with it results so acceptable to the writers of the day.

The social consequence of men of letters followed immediately upon the recognition of their political importance. Men of literary genius were not only patronized by, but were brought into familiar intercourse with, the leading Ministers as well as with the chiefs of the Opposition. Literary men were found occupying government posts. Prior and Gay were employed on important embassies, Addison became a Secretary of State, Swift was the trusted adviser of Oxford and of Bolingbroke.

The internal history of England from 1688 to 1727 was exceptionally exciting. The Revolution followed by the unpopular measures of William, the struggles in connection with the Peace of Utrecht, the uncertainty hanging over the Succession, and the opposition of a large portion of the population to George I., gave great opportunities to essayists, pamphleteers, and poets. The absence of a daily press, of public meetings, and of extended electoral campaigns at a period when party interests ran high and the popular excitement was intense, produced a crowd of writers of political tracts. No Minister could disdain their aid, when it was only by means of such pamphlets and broadsides that he could guide or educate public opinion. Defoe had already distinguished himself as William III.'s adjutant. He had, in a stirring pamphlet, shown that a standing army is not inconsistent with a free Government. A few years later he stood in the pillory for his *Shortest Way with the Dissenters ;* a fine species of irony not appreciated by the High Church party, who were by it recommended to hang any Dissenter found in a Conventicle. Oxford and Bolingbroke saw at once the immense importance of securing the ablest political writers of their day. Swift's articles in the *Examiner,* his *Conduct of the Allies,* and his *Remarks upon the Barrier Treaty,* completely revolutionized opinion in England with regard to the war. His *Public Spirit of the Whigs* was an answer to Steele's *Crisis.* The *Review* appeared in 1704, and supported, as a rule, whatever Government was in power. The *Examiner,* a Thursday weekly paper, founded by Bolingbroke, with the aid of Atterbury, Prior, and Dr. Freind, in the autumn of 1710, was opposed the same year by the *Whig Examiner,* edited by Addison.

Each side, too, had its own poets. When Addison, the Whig poet-laureate, and the friend of Halifax, wrote the *Campaign* in honour of the victory of Blenheim, Bolingbroke at once employed John Philips, the author of *The Splendid Shilling,* and of *Cyder,* to write his *Blenheim.* Literature and politics were indeed closely intertwined, and it was always Bolingbroke's aim to shine as a leader in literature no less than in politics. His relations throughout his life with the great literary giants of the day bring out the most pleasing side of his character, and give us glimpses of the most delightful portions of his life. Even before his entry into Parliament he had aspired to be a poet. He had formed Dryden's acquaintance, and had written some verses eulogistic of his translation of Virgil. He patronized, as we have seen, John Philips, a poet who died in 1708, at the early age of thirty-three, and who ended his *Blenheim* with some lines on the Manor House of Bucklersbury:

> " Thus from the noisy crowd exempt, with ease
> And plenty blest, amid the mazy groves,
> Sweet solitude ! Where warbling birds provoke
> The silent muse, delicious rural seat
> Of St. John, English Memmius, I presumed
> To sing Britannic trophies, inexpert
> Of war, with mean attempt."

During the years of his Secretaryship, the literary circle with which he associated contained, among others, Swift, Pope, Congreve, Parnell, Arbuthnot, Prior, and Gay. Most, if not all, of them were members of the Society of Brothers, and later of the famous Scriblerus Club.

Pope, whose acquaintance with Bolingbroke was to lead to such momentous results, was introduced to him by Swift. The great Doctor had been pleased with the poet's *Windsor Castle*, which appeared in March, 1713, and in which Pope sneered at the Revolution, declared enthusiastically for the Peace, and wrote a flattering dedication to Bolingbroke. Even in those busy days, Bolingbroke undertook to correct portions of the *Translation of the Iliad*, at which Pope was then working. The appearance of the first volume, however, found Bolingbroke in exile, Oxford in prison, and Swift in Ireland. By his leaning towards the Tories in his *Windsor Castle*, Pope had offended his old Whig friends, and had been attacked in an underhand manner in the *Guardian*. His recompense for his partial alienation from the Whig coterie, and for his abandonment of his original intention to keep clear from politics, was that friendship with Bolingbroke, which grew into the devotion of a life.

Swift and Prior saw probably more of Bolingbroke than the others, as in their respective ways they were both occupied in giving very valuable aid to the Government. One of the accusations brought afterwards against Prior and Bolingbroke was that they had been unseasonably witty during the most serious and solemn negotiations. Swift had been introduced by Oxford to Bolingbroke in October, 1710, and, as has been seen, speedily became a political power on the Tory side. He soon grew very intimate with the leading Ministers, and his *Journal to Stella* is full of most valuable political and social information. He has left a very interesting sketch of St. John's character as it appeared to him in the autumn of 1711.

"I think Mr. St. John," he writes, "the greatest young man I ever knew; wit, capacity, beauty, quickness of apprehension, good learning, and an excellent taste; the best orator in the House of Commons, admirable conversation, good nature, and good manners; generous, and a despiser of money. His only fault is talking to his friends in way of complaint of too great a load of business, which looks a little like affectation; and he endeavours too much to mix the fine gentleman and man of pleasure with the man of business."

As early as February, 1711, he had been admitted to Harley's regular Saturday dinners, where Harley and St. John both addressed him as Jonathan. Swift's alliance with the Tories marks the time when the power of the Press in England was greater than at any previous period, and when political writers for the first time ceased to be mere hirelings, and became the intimates of Ministers. " I dined to-day with Mr. Secretary St. John," wrote Swift in these years of his prosperity: " I went to the Court of Requests at noon, and sent Mr. Harley into the House to call the Secretary, and let him know I would not dine with him if he dined late." From the beginning of 1711, too, Swift began to dine with Bolingbroke every Sunday, and during the summer months of 1711, when the Queen's residence at Windsor necessitated St. John's presence there every other Sunday, Swift not unfrequently visited him. Sometimes Bolingbroke broke his journey at Peterborough House. On September the 1st, 1711, he and Swift dined there in Peterborough's absence—the occasion when Swift was much struck with the kitchen-garden. "It is," he wrote, "the finest fruit garden I have ever seen about this town, and abundance of hot walls for grapes, which are ripening fast."

The second period in Bolingbroke's literary career may be said to date from his return from exile. During this period he had more leisure and more time to consider political, philosophical, and religious questions. He was older, he had gained more experience; his residence at La Source had resulted in much mental activity. On his return to England, in 1725, Dawley became the centre of a literary circle, which included for a time Pope, Swift, Gay, and Voltaire. Dawley itself was a fine, spacious residence, situated in the village of Harlington, near Uxbridge, fourteen miles from London and one mile from the Bath Road. The Manor House was taken down in 1780. There, in Bolingbroke's own words, "he was in a hermitage where no man came but for the sake of the hermit": for then he found "that the insects, which used to hum and buzz about him in the sunshine, fled to men of more prosperous fortune, and forsook him when in the shade." There his life at Bucklersbury, in the years 1708 and 1709, was reproduced in many of its features. True, he still took an interest in politics, and during the greater part of his residence at Dawley was busy organizing attacks on Walpole in *The Craftsman*, and within the walls of Parliament. But during intervals of the struggle, as, for example, in 1728, after the failure of his hopes to see Walpole ruined upon the accession of George II., he lived the life of a country gentleman, devoting himself on the one hand to study, and on the other to farming and hunting. On June the 28th, 1728, Pope wrote from Dawley to Swift a letter which is often quoted :—

"I now hold the pen for my Lord Bolingbroke, who is reading your letter between two haycocks ; but his attention is somewhat diverted by casting his eyes on the clouds, not in admiration of what you say, but for fear of a shower. . . . As to the return of his health and vigour, were you here, you might inquire of his haymakers ; but, as to his temperance, I can answer that (for one whole day) we have had nothing for dinner but mutton broth, beans and bacon, and a barndoor fowl. Now his lordship is run after his cart, I have a moment left to myself to tell you that I overheard him yesterday agree with a painter for £200 to paint his country hall with trophies of ricks, spades, prongs, etc., and other ornaments, merely," added the poet maliciously, " 'to countenance his calling this place a farm.' "

But it is in its relation to Bolingbroke's intellectual influence that this handsome country-house has become so widely known. Dawley was within a pleasant ride from Twickenham, where Pope had lived since 1718, and Dawley and Twickenham both became literary centres, the fame of which will live long in the history of English literature.

Time had already laid its hand on many of the members of that brilliant circle which had gathered round Boling-broke during the last years of Anne's reign. Atterbury was an exile, Prior and Parnell were both dead. At Dawley and Twickenham, however, the survivors of that circle and of that celebrated literary association, the Scriblerus Club, again came together. The year 1725 and the next few years were to make many of those survivors famous. The year 1725 marks the beginning of that period in Pope's literary career in which the works he composed are his greatest in "sheer literary power." In 1727 three volumes of his *Miscellanies*, followed in 1728 by *The Dunciad*, showed the world the strength of Pope's satire. In 1726 Swift was at Dawley and Twickenham, and on July the 7th Pope entertained at a dinner, which may be termed historical, Congreve, Bolingbroke, Gay, and Swift, who had lately arrived from Ireland bringing with him the manuscript of *Gulliver's Travels*, which in 1727 was published anonymously. At the end of May, 1726, Voltaire arrived in England, and at once renewed the acquaintance he had made with Bolingbroke at La Source in 1721. That Statesman in 1727 wrote the *Vision of Camelick* in the *Craftsman*, and further attacked Walpole in the first number of the *Occasional Writer*. In 1728 Gay's *Beggars' Opera* was produced, over the success of which the inmates of Dawley rejoiced.

What a picture is presented to us! Bolingbroke affecting to be merely interested in country pursuits, and rarely mentioning politics when conversing with his friends, but still burning with restless ambition, and sparing no pains to secure Walpole's downfall; Swift busy with his charming satire, which was to secure an instantaneous and permanent popularity; Voltaire correcting his *Henriade*, which he at first intended to dedicate to Bolingbroke; and which, having already appeared in 1723 as *La Ligue*, was published in March, 1728; Arbuthnot, Gay, and Pope full of plans for revenge on the miserable Whig writers, the result of their deliberations being *The Dunciad*. Powerful as *The Dunciad* is, it belongs to a far lower level of poetry than *The Essay on Criticism* and *The Rape of the Lock*, which had already won for Pope a foremost place among living English poets.

The establishment of Bolingbroke in Pope's neighbourhood resulted, not only in a warm friendship between the two men, but enabled Bolingbroke to influence beneficially the genius of Pope. The correspondence of Bolingbroke and Pope with Swift gives a pleasant idea of their mutual relations, and of their friendship with Arbuthnot, Gay, and Congreve. Any one who reads those letters will emphatically endorse Leslie Stephen's assertion, " that there is scarcely a more interesting volume in the language than that which contains the correspondence of Swift, Bolingbroke, and Pope " (*Pope*, by Leslie Stephen, p. 156).

Swift's dislike to his residence in Ireland gives his letters a bitter turn : " I reckon no man is thoroughly miserable unless he be condemned to dwell in Ireland," he had written some sixteen years previously, and he continued to hold the same views. He took, however, great interest in the doings of his friends in England, though he only crossed over from Dublin twice during the period, in 1726, and for the last time in 1727. He was delighted at the success of Gay's opera, he was impatient to see *The Dunciad ;* he regarded Bolingbroke, Pope, and himself as " a peculiar triumvirate, who have nothing to expect or to fear." But his letters are those of an avowed misanthrope. Everything had gone wrong with him, his friends were either dead or far away, his health was rapidly declining, his hopes of English preferment on the death of George I. had been dashed to the ground, and he had now returned to Ireland to leave it no more. In 1729 he wrote to Bolingbroke :—

" ' You think, as I ought to think, that it is time for me to have done with the world ; and so I would, if I could get into a better before I was called into the best, and not die here in a rage, like a poisoned rat in a hole.' "

His sorrows and despondency colour the whole of his correspondence with his old friends, and increase till death in October, 1745, withdraws from life's stage that stern humorist, who had played so important a part during the period when Bolingbroke's star was in the ascendant. He rose with Bolingbroke to a political importance never before realized by a man of letters. After the death of Anne, though, like Bolingbroke, he secured certain political successes, as in the case of Wood's Halfpence, he never mixed again with members of Cabinets or advised Ministers on questions of policy.

Bolingbroke's correspondence is of an entirely different character. Though, like Swift, cut off from any active share in politics, though like him a disappointed man, though similarly bristling with keen prejudices, his letters have no despairing tone. Leslie Stephen describes in some admirable words the effect upon the reader of a perusal of Bolingbroke's letters to Swift and Pope :—

"We see through Bolingbroke's magnificent self-deceit ; the flowing manners of the statesman, who, though the game is lost, is longing for a favourable turn of the card, but still affects to solace himself with philosophy, and wraps himself in dignified reflections upon the blessings of retirement, contrast with Swift's downright avowal of indignant scorn for himself and mankind" (*Pope*, by Leslie Stephen, p. 157).

Pope's letters are, as might be expected, characterized by hypocrisy, sympathy with his friends, and great admiration for Bolingbroke. Of the three friends, Pope was during these years alone successful. His frequent declarations of indifference to the applause of the world came strangely from a man who was above all men most keenly desirous of fame and sensitive of adverse criticism. His worship of Bolingbroke was sincere. At one time he writes that "it looks as if that great man had been placed here by mistake." And he continues that, "when the comet appeared a month or two ago, I sometimes fancied that it might be come to carry him home, as a coach comes to one's door for other visitors." And later he begs Swift to argue Bolingbroke out of his fruitless interference with politics, and complains that that statesman is so taken up with particular men, that he neglects mankind, and is still a creature of the world, not of the universe.

Meanwhile the genius of Pope, which had just shown its power of direct satire in *The Dunciad*, fell under the influence of Bolingbroke.

"Between 1732 and 1740," says De Quincey, "he was chiefly engaged in satires, which uniformly speak a high moral tone in the midst of personal invective ; or in poems directly philosophical, which almost as uniformly speak the bitter tone of satire in the midst of dispassionate ethics."

His *Essay on Man* was undertaken at the instigation of Bolingbroke, who showed the greatest interest in the work. In Pope's garden at Twickenham he had already frequently conversed with him on philosophic subjects, and further, in order to make clear his meaning, Bolingbroke described, in an enormous number of letters or essays to Pope, his philosophic system.

"Does Pope talk to you," writes Bolingbroke to Swift in 1731, "of the noble work which, at my instigation, he has begun in such a manner that he must be convinced by this time I judged better of his talents than he did?"

While the *Essay on Man* was still in progress, Pope wrote the *Moral Essays*, which Bolingbroke, in a letter to Swift, describes as a fine work, and in its way superior to Horace. The first of the four epistles which composed the *Essay on Man* appeared in 1733, and the other parts followed during 1733 and 1734. In them religion is put on a rational basis, and Bolingbroke's sentiments find full expression throughout the whole poem. Between 1735 and 1738, in the *Satires and Epistles of Horace Imitated*, Pope attacked violently the followers of Walpole. These satires and epistles form, it has been said, "a concentrated essence of the bitterness of the Opposition." Pope made no secret of his obligations to Bolingbroke. His admiration for that statesman and his writings remained unchecked till death came in 1744 to sever one of the most famous literary friendships on record. In 1738 Bolingbroke, during a visit to England, spent some time at Twickenham, and in the next year Pope wrote an account of his doings to Swift, then in his declining years:

"He has sold Dawley for £26,000, much to his own satisfaction. His plan of life is now a very agreeable one; in the finest country of France, divided between study and exercise, for he still reads and writes five or six hours a day, and generally hunts twice a week. He has the whole forest of Fontainebleau at his command, with the King's stables and dogs, etc., his lady's son-in-law being governor of the place. . . . I never saw him in stronger health, or in better humour with his friends, or more indifferent and dispassionate to his enemies. . . . We often commemorated you during the five months we lived together at Twickenham, at which place could I see you again, as I hope to see him, I would envy no country in the world."

The complete ascendancy which Bolingbroke had gained during his residence at Dawley over Pope is well illustrated by a letter written by the poet shortly after Wyndham's death. In it he assures Bolingbroke that England can now be saved only by his ability. And his resolution to return to England, should it be necessary, he styles as being " not patriotism, but downright piety." Little less than canonization would, in his opinion, be fitting for such a man.

To Bolingbroke Pope's death was a great blow. For upwards of twenty years they had been the closest friends, seeing much of one another, engaged in similar works, holding the same views. Bolingbroke's influence had done much for Pope, and the sensitive Pope had repaid the debt by persuading Bolingbroke to withdraw his exclusive interest in politics and " low ambitions." Pope loved fame ; Bolingbroke enabled him to produce the *Essay on Man*. Pope enjoyed revenge ; Bolingbroke's suggestion that he should write the *Imitations of Horace* was carried out with triumphant success. On the other hand, the close intimacy with the poet had a corresponding effect on the statesman. Bolingbroke's *Epistolary Essays* were written in answer to Pope's appeal, and Bolingbroke's great interest in the higher regions of thought during these years was in no small measure due to the presence of an enthusiastic disciple. Bolingbroke's influence over Pope was exercised principally by means of conversation. " His manner of speaking in private conversation," says Chesterfield, " is as full and elegant as his writings." Voltaire had already felt the influence of these conversations.

The author of the *Henriade* first met Bolingbroke at La Source in 1721, and was profoundly impressed by his host's philosophical and historical ideas. Bolingbroke had pleased him by placing *La Ligue* at the head of French poetry, and Voltaire became then, like Pope later, an eager disciple of the English statesman. In 1724 Bolingbroke writes from France to Pope, that he is reading Voltaire's *Death of Mariamne*, which was to be played that Lent, and that Voltaire hopes soon to introduce himself to Pope. This introduction took place in 1726, when Voltaire paid his first visit to England. Before that visit, Pope, not being a French scholar, had with difficulty read *La Ligue*, and had written to Bolingbroke, praising the poem in a qualified manner : " I cannot," he says, " pretend to judge with any exactness of the beauties of a foreign language which I understand but imperfectly."

The circumstances under which the young François Arouet paid his celebrated visit to England tended to heighten his admiration for much that he saw and heard. Twice had he tasted of the Bastille, the first time (1716) his imprisonment being the result of a poem commenting upon the social abuses of the day. The Government of the Regent, which is supposed by some to have inaugurated a reaction from the despotism of Louis XIV., was not going to allow without protest a criticism of the social and governmental evils under which France was then groaning. The young Arouet was therefore shut up in the Bastille on the suspicion of being the author of the poem. His challenge of the Chevalier de Rohan for an insult was answered by another imprisonment followed by an injunction to leave Paris. With a keen sense of the disadvantages of living under a tyrannical government, Voltaire, as he is now called, came to England. " He left France," says Lord Morley, " a poet ; he returned to it a sage."

He arrived in England just before the blighting influence of Walpole's government had fallen upon the men of letters. The brilliant group of the Queen Anne men, though sadly decimated, was still in existence. The close connection between literature and politics continued, and the contrast between the state of things in France, where a poet was caned by a nobleman's lackey, and the feeling in England, which rewarded poetic ability with political posts and with well-endowed sinecures, was thoroughly appreciated by the author of the *Henriade*.

None the less striking to the French poet was the, to him, extraordinary liberty enjoyed by the Press. He saw a people not only saying what they pleased, but printing without let or hindrance the most direct personal attacks on the Ministers and the most scathing criticisms on their policy. He perceived that invectives against the religion of the country were permitted, and that new religious and philosophical theories could be freely propounded. Not even the sovereign could escape from openly expressed criticism. Then, again, he found that exemption of certain classes from taxation—that curse of ancient France—did not exist in England. All that is implied in the terms constitutional freedom, liberty of the Press and of the subject, equality of taxation, mixture of ranks, nobility of labour, came more or less as a revelation to Voltaire.

Till 1729 Voltaire lived almost entirely in England. A very interesting account of his residence here, and an estimate of Bolingbroke's influence on his writings is to be found in the late Mr. Churton Collins' essay on *Voltaire in England*. After the publication of the *Henriade* he began, at the instigation of Bolingbroke, the *Tragedy of Brutus*, which when completed, he dedicated to that statesman. He was at the same time working at his history of Charles XII., and collecting materials for his history of Louis XIV. But, while producing, he was busy accumulating with a zest that is simply astounding. He plunged into the study of all branches of English literature; poetry, history, theology, natural science, and philosophy. He read Shakespeare, Milton, and Dryden most carefully. His admiration for

Pope's poetry was unbounded, and he considered Addison's *Cato* a fine production. The works of Waller, Prior, Congreve, Wycherley, Vanbrugh, and Rochester were all devoured, and he took an especial interest in *Hudibras*, so seldom read at the present day. He had unusual advantages for obtaining special information on English Constitutional history, and facts for his histories of the Great French and Swedish Monarchs. Though he apparently made Dawley his headquarters, he also stayed with Peterborough, and Bubb Doddington. At one or other of the houses of his friends he made the acquaintance of Swift, and of Congreve, of Gay, and of Young; with the Dowager Duchess of Marlborough he discussed Louis XIV. and Charles XII.

Most of his views on the political condition of England, on its institutions, and on the spirit of its laws are largely affected by the opinions of Bolingbroke, who held, during the period of his residence at Dawley, that a corrupt oligarchy was transforming the old free English institutions into a government, the aim of which was to advance party at the expense of national interests. Hence Bolingbroke's complaints about the decadence of the spirit of liberty misled Voltaire, who in consequence failed to understand the real character of the Revolution of 1688. His observations on English political life, contained in his *Letters on the English*, written before he left England, presented such a contrast to the state of things existing in France, that they were ordered to be burnt in 1734. It is probably owing to Bolingbroke's influence that they are wanting in any adequate account of our political liberties, and entirely fail to show that the author had grasped the importance of the English free constitutional forms.

In Voltaire's religious and philosophic studies the influence which Bolingbroke had already exercised at La Source was developed and largely amplified. From Bolingbroke Voltaire had derived the rationalistic spirit.

It was at La Source that Bolingbroke finished his *Letters to M. de Pouilly;* he was also busy writing the *Reflections on Innate Moral Principles* while Voltaire was his guest. When they again met at Dawley the seed already sown was beginning to bear fruit, and Voltaire found frequent opportunities of continuing his discussions. In England the opinions of the Deists were being much canvassed, and Bolingbroke was a Deist. "It is not too much to say," writes Lord Morley, "that Bolingbroke was the direct progenitor of Voltaire's opinions in religion." Voltaire, who had read Locke, now studied the Deistical controversy which was raging, and read the works of such men as Toland and Collins, Shaftesbury, and Chubb. From them, through, as it were, the medium of Bolingbroke, Voltaire gradually formed his religious philosophy. These studies he continued in France in after years, and throughout his writings, which so profoundly affected the thought of Europe and to some extent the political action of France, the influence of Bolingbroke can be constantly discerned.

As we study with intense interest the literature and politics in Bolingbroke's days, we are tempted to look back to the times of Lorenzo de' Medici, under whose sway Florentine society, like English Society under Queen Anne and George I., was largely affected by politics and literature. In Florence, as in England, men delighted in literary and philosophical conversation. At Dawley and Twickenham, just as in the Ruccellai Gardens, men met together in social clubs, which often had a political and philosophical character. The death of Lorenzo heralded the enslavement of Italy; even before Bolingbroke's death, the tendencies of the age had shrivelled up the literary aspirations, and with them had brought to an end the literary friendships of one of the most interesting periods of English literar history.

CHAPTER X

BOLINGBROKE'S POLITICAL, PHILOSOPHICAL, AND THEOLOGICAL OPINIONS.

Note on his political writings—Charge of inconsistency—His political aims in Anne's reign—His short period of Jacobitism—His political theories when opposing Walpole—*The Dissertation on Parties*—His reconstruction of Toryism—*The Patriot King*—Its effect on the policy of George III. and on the future of Toryism—Bolingbroke a democratic Tory—Lord Beaconsfield's opinion as to the value of his services to the Tory party—Bolingbroke's philosophical and religious opinions—His writings—Their uncritical and unhistorical character—Opinion of Lechler—The principles of the Deistic writers well illustrated from Bolingbroke's writings—Contempt for all dogmatic theologians—Importance of reason—Memory—Influence of the rationalistic point of view upon psychology—Bolingbroke's treatment of ethics and theology—His political theory.

THE political opinions of Bolingbroke are in part of little permanent value, being for the most part written in the heat of exciting party struggles. To two classes of persons his writings appeal. The admirer of eloquent expression and of splendid diction will read Bolingbroke's writings. He will find there the inexhaustible resources of the English language ; he will learn how varied, how flexible, how dignified it becomes in the hand of a master. He will find there the perfection of English prose ; he will appreciate the undefinable influence of style. The historical student will find in his political writings the explanations of much that would otherwise be inexplicable.[1]

---

[1] Bolingbroke's political opinions are to be gathered from :—

    (1) His political correspondence during the time he was Secretary of State, which is our principal guide to the policy of the Ministry during the negotiations of the Peace of Utrecht.

Bolingbroke, it must never be forgotten, always threw himself heart and soul into the questions which were immediately pressing for solution. It has been well said of him that he was " a consummate master of political strategy, as well as a great Constitutional moralist " (*Bolingbroke*, by Harrop, p. 25). As soon as fresh problems appeared or a fresh development in politics took place, he at once boldly examined the situation and came forward with a programme, without apparently any regard for consistency. He had a wonderful knack of adapting himself to fresh circumstances, and, with the keen eye of a man accustomed to move behind the scenes of political life, of choosing the right watchword by which a defeated party might be rallied. It is often

---

(2) His contributions to *The Craftsman*—the principal of which in their collected form are known as *Remarks on the History of England* and the *Dissertation on Parties*—are most valuable aids to our knowledge of the domestic politics of the day.

(3) A variety of dissertations and essays, partly purely historical, partly merely political.

Of the historical dissertations, the *Letter to Sir William Wyndham*, written in 1717, but not published till 1753, is perhaps the most celebrated. In most points the statements are trustworthy, and it forms a very interesting chapter of history. Next in importance come the letters on *The Study of History*, of which the first five point out that history should be studied philosophically ; the sixth and seventh give a summary of the course of English history in the sixteenth and seventeenth, and early years of the eighteenth centuries ; the eighth is a defence of the Peace of Utrecht. In 1749 he wrote the dissertation on the *State of Parties at the Accession of George I*. The essays in which he deals more especially with political theory are : *The Letters on the Spirit of Patriotism, The Patriot King*, and *The Dissertation on Parties*. Of these, the influence of *The Patriot King*, which was published in 1749, was immense on that and the next generation, and is seen in many of Lord Beaconsfield's ideas and not unfrequently in his language. All Bolingbroke's writings mentioned in this chapter are to be found in his collected works, and all references are to the 1809 edition, in eight volumes.

(4) A great number of letters, or which the most important are to be found in the *Marchmont Papers*.

pointed out how the policy of a coalition against Walpole was directly opposed to his policy of Tory consolidation under Anne. Hence he is usually accused of inconsistency and insincerity. Such charges show a want of knowledge of the character and tendency of the political movements under Anne and her two successors.

During the last four years of Anne's reign, Bolingbroke certainly employed all his efforts in opposition to Oxford, who, like Marlborough, loved divided administrations, to make the lines between parties as clear as possible, and to form a strong united Tory Ministry. To establish the Government on a Tory basis was an intelligible policy. The overthrow of the Whig influence was to be accomplished by means of the authority of the Queen, supported by the will of the people. Coalitions, the object of Oxford's policy, must be discarded for ever. No terms were to be made with political opponents. By a policy of proscription and exclusion, that is, by a series of Acts brought forward and carried in a constitutional manner, all the governing power was to be placed in the hands of the High Church party. The majority of the nation was decidedly Tory, and the nation must be appealed to. Swift held similar views, and *The Conduct of the Allies* marks the first definite attempt in English political life to appeal to public opinion. That this policy was primarily in the interest of the Church and the landed gentry is not to be denied, and in his *Letter to Sir William Wyndham* his political theories during these years are clearly described.

After his exile, which included a desperate attempt to restore Jacobitism, he entered upon a new struggle under fresh circumstances. He was again opposed to the Whigs, who now, supported by the Sovereign and headed by a sagacious Minister, governed the country. He accordingly devoted himself to the difficult task of making the Hanoverian Tories and Jacobites recognize the existing dynasty, and of persuading the Malcontent Whigs that their former opponents had given up their Jacobite doctrines. Walpole was firmly established in power, and was carrying out in the interest of his followers that policy of proscription and exclusion formerly advocated by Bolingbroke. While engaged in the difficult task of conciliating the Malcontent Whigs Bolingbroke professed himself a warm advocate of the Revolution principles, but deprecated the system of Government by party, and the substitution of a united Cabinet for the ancient Royal Council. He consistently pointed out that the choice before the electors was between Oligarchy and Democracy. He thus threw aside his former opinions, his ancient belief in the existence of strong party divisions ; in their stead he advocated a Coalition. In his *Dissertation on Parties* he points out that the old political divisions have lost their meaning, that the old " associations of ideas " are broken, that new combinations had forced themselves into notice ;

"that it would be as absurd to impute to the Tories the principles which were laid to their charge formerly as it would be to ascribe to the projector (Walpole) and his faction the name of Whigs, while they daily forfeit that character by their actions" (vol. iii. p. 39).

The Revolution Settlement is now secure, the new dynasty is generally recognized. But a fresh danger has arisen. " King William defended us from Popery and slavery," after the Revolution had saved us from the attempt of James to increase his prerogative. The object of the Revolution was plainly designated to restore and secure our Government, ecclesiastical and civil, on true foundations (vol. iii. p. 171). But certain defects in our constitution not noticed in 1688-9 have become dangerous. The design of the Revolution could not be accomplished unless " the freedom of elections and the frequency, integrity, and independence of Parliaments were sufficiently provided for " (vol. iii. p. 177). Walpole and his faction, by discrediting the Tories, keep themselves in power. This perpetuated power leads to corruption. To such an extent had corruption grown, that the "independency of Parliament, in which the essence of our constitution, and by consequence of our liberty, consists, seems to be in great, not to say in imminent, danger of being lost" (vol. iii. p. 277).

With these "high sentiments of constitutional morality" in his pamphlets, Bolingbroke appealed to the conservative instincts of the people against dangerous and pernicious innovations. In a very striking letter to Lord Polwarth in July, 1739, after Walpole had been in office nearly twenty years, he despaired of saving the independence of Parliament. An Administration on what he calls a national basis would alone restore that independence: for then the people would be able to insist on their right "to preserve that fundamental principle of their free constitution of Government" (*Marchmont Papers*, vol. ii. p. 191).

As long as Bolingbroke lived, he could not break through the Whig phalanx. With all their faults, England owes a debt of gratitude to the great Whig families. Their administrative powers were admirable; they had the interest of the country at heart; they established the Hanoverian dynasty firmly on the throne; under them, the elder Pitt carried on a successful war, resulting in the establishment of England's Empire; the country had never been so uniformly prosperous, the division between rich and poor had rarely been so slight as during the reigns of the first two Georges, when the Revolution families governed. But by George III.'s accession the new professional politician, a Whig parasite, belonging to a class admirably described by Sir George Trevelyan in his *Early History of Charles James Fox*, had entered upon the Whig heritage. The Whig party, undermined by corruption, the result of long tenure of power, had split into sections. George III.'s policy was to put into practice the views of Bolingbroke as expressed in the *Dis-*

sertation on Parties, and in his letter to Polwarth, and to preserve the Constitution by establishing a Government independent of party, on a national basis. He wished to be a king in reality, not merely in name ; a patriot king after the pattern drawn by Bolingbroke.

We have seen in a former chapter how it came to pass that Bolingbroke's political ideas, described above, were never put into force during his lifetime. His second, and this time self-imposed exile, in 1735 marks the failure of the third phase of his political ideas. He had *first*, between 1710 and 1714, attempted, without abolishing the Act of Settlement, to replace the Tory party in that position of supremacy which it enjoyed at the time of the Revolution of 1688 ; he had *secondly*, in 1715, aided in an unsuccessful attempt to restore Jacobitism and overthrow the Act of Settlement. He had, *thirdly*, failed, after a gallant effort, to abolish party distinctions by means of a coalition of all parties. He now, after having broken with Pulteney and the Malcontent Whigs, entered upon the *fourth* phase of his political ideas, adopted in some respects a new political theory, and attempted to reconstruct Toryism on the basis of patriotism. *The Patriot King* expresses this theory, and, on its publication in 1749, became widely known. It appeals to all who hate the name of party and dislike the existence of party government. According to the system of government sketched out in this treatise, " a limited monarchy is the best of governments," and a hereditary monarchy of monarchies. " The good of the people is the ultimate and true end of Government," and " the greatest good of a people is their liberty." The best way to provide for the continuance of that liberty is by securing the accession of a patriot king, who will not be a sovereign by divine right, nor the mere figure-head of a Government directed by an oligarchy. He will be a constitutional sovereign, whose power is limited by his consent to exercise that power subject to public opinion expressed in a free Parliament. Under him corruption will cease, for a patriot king has no reason to be corrupt.

"He is the most powerful of all reformers, for he is himself a sort of standing miracle so rarely seen, and so little understood, that the sure effects of his appearance will be admiration and love in every honest breast, confusion and terror to every guilty conscience, but submission and resignation in all" (vol. iv., p. 273).

In writing *The Patriot King*, Bolingbroke was advancing political theories to some extent similar to those laid down in the *Dissertation on Parties*. His immediate object at the time was to establish his position with Frederick, the Prince of Wales, and to checkmate Pulteney and his followers, who had just wrecked his scheme of a Coalition. That all the views expressed in *The Patriot King* could ever be realized hardly needs demonstration. Where was the king to be found who would act the part described? Even supposing that one prince of ability conformed to the requirements set forth in this treatise, what guarantee would there be that his successors would follow in his footsteps? Was it really likely that corruption and party spirit would disappear before this magic centre? Nor can Bolingbroke explain satisfactorily the steps in the transformation of Parliamentary Government into a national council existing without parties. In spite of all these difficulties the fact remains that his famous essay became a real force in political life, a mighty lever which largely contributed to the ruin of the Venetian oligarchy. By its aid George III. smote the Whigs hip and thigh, and for ten years, without, indeed, rising to the sublime height of *The Patriot King*, carried out in certain points some of the principles laid down in that famous treatise.

Thus it came about that the object at which Bolingbroke had aimed all his life and by various methods, was attained by his means after his death. *The Patriot King* very largely aided in the reconstruction of that Tory party which found leaders in Bute, North, the younger Pitt, and Disraeli. In a critical estimate of the causes of the successful assertion by the Tories of their right to a share in the Government of the country in the reign of George III., *The Patriot King* occupies with regard to public opinion a position similar to that of *The Conduct of the Allies*. In each case the popular feeling which had already declared itself was powerfully fostered and accelerated by these respective treatises. In 1710 the people were, for several well-known reasons, weary of the Whig Government, and Swift's writings not only strengthened them in their desire to end the war, but also expressed what was the general view. " Many of " the elder Pitt's " utterances were," writes Mr. Grant Robertson, " strongly tinged with Bolingbroke's ideas, which identified party with faction, and aimed at breaking up the prevailing system and machinery."[1] On George III.'s accession Parliament had ceased to represent the people, and had become factious and corrupt. *The Patriot King* became the watchword for the literary class, who never had any sympathy with Walpole's system of Government, for the Tories, who wished after their long exclusion from the Government to again direct affairs, for Whigs like Pitt, who hated the party system, and for George III., who was determined to free himself from the thraldom of the Whig families.

The strength of the Whig position lay in this, that they had made the executive practically responsible to Parliament. But, while securing in great measure the direction of affairs, they had endeavoured to make their position safe by controlling the members of Parliament, and the elections to Parliament, by means of corruption. They failed to see the advantage of a Parliament responsible to the people. They were anxious to govern in the interest of the nation,

[1] C. Grant Robertson, *England under the Hanoverians*, p. 138. London : Methuen and Co.

but they did not permit the nation to exercise any control over, or to possess any influence in Parliament. The abuses to which such a system was liable were obvious, and these were violently attacked by Bolingbroke in the palmy days of Whig ascendancy. The publication of *The Patriot King* found Walpole's system in a state of decay, and Parliament the battle-ground of various small bodies of self-seeking politicians. Is it to be wondered at if Tories like Johnson despised Whiggism, which under "the Pelhams was no better than the politics of stock-jobbers, and the religion of infidels," and believed that a Prince who pursued the "interest of his people could not fail of Parliamentary concurrence"? In spite, then, of many manifest absurdities, *The Patriot King* was immediately popular because it struck a national chord, and expressed a widespread feeling of discontent.

We have lastly to summarize Bolingbroke's political views, and to consider shortly the direct bearing of his political theories on the future of the Tory party. We have seen the *four phases* through which his political opinions passed. In each phase he adapted his views to a special contingency ; but one principle runs throughout his political writings, the principle, namely, of strengthening the Crown by popular safeguards. Bolingbroke was never a Tory in the sense that Rochester, or Bute, or North, or Eldon were Tories. The Toryism of his day was largely tinged with Jacobitism, and, even if opposed to the return of the Pretender, never shook itself quite clear from divine right, passive obedience, and the like. Bolingbroke was always ahead of his party. In his first Parliament he had seen Harley, who had no sympathy with high monarchical doctrines, compel the Tory party to pass the Act of Settlement and the Abjuration Bill. He never seems to have entirely discarded this popular form of Toryism then adopted by Harley ; he ridiculed divine right ; he always hated a

Venetian oligarchy, and, in opposition to Walpole's system, pressed for the greater independence of the House of Commons. *The Patriot King* was to be subjected to public opinion as manifested in a free territorial Parliament of landlords chosen by widest suffrage.

In fact, there was a good deal of the democratic Tory about Bolingbroke. " Good government depends, under our constitution, on the unity of interest between the King and his subjects," he had written some years before the appearance of *The Patriot King*, and, in doing so, had appealed to a sentiment which was destined to become a mighty force after his own death. George III., in establishing the power of the Crown against Parliament and in reducing his ministers to the position of mere agents and advisers, was acting as much in harmony with the wish of the people as with the political theories of Bolingbroke. After the American War the Whigs again came into power, but they had not learnt wisdom during adversity. Dreading the influence of the Crown and ignoring the popular feeling, they ruined themselves for some fifty years by their fatal Coalition with Lord North. Pitt's policy of appealing from a selfish oligarchy to the mass of the voters and of establishing, by means of a beneficent policy, good relations between the Crown and the people, was a practical expression of Bolingbroke's political opinions.

The success of Bolingbroke's reconstruction of Toryism was well described by Disraeli in 1835 :

" He eradicated from Toryism all their absurd and odious doctrines which Toryism had adventitiously adopted, clearly developed its essential and permanent character, discarded *jure divino*, demolished passive obedience, threw to the winds the doctrine of non-resistance, placed the abolition of James, and the accession of George on their right bases, and, in the complete reorganization of the public mind, laid the foundation for the future accession of the Tory party to power, and to that popular and triumphant career which must ever await the policy of an administration inspired by the spirit of our free and ancient institutions."

Disraeli, unlike Burke, fully appreciated and acknowledged the debt which he owed to Bolingbroke. " Many of his (Disraeli's) telling phrases . . . are derived from Bolingbroke. His constitutional theories . . . are Bolingbroke's ; so were his foreign and fiscal policies."[1] His attitude towards the Ministry during the Crimean War and the Danish War of 1864 has been compared to that of Bolingbroke in 1729.

The philosophical and religious opinions of Lord Bolingbroke are now of comparatively little importance, either in the history of philosophy and theology or in the history of the life of their author. They are to be found in the last three volumes of Mallet's edition of his works. The Essays, in which they are embodied, are addressed to Alexander Pope, and were all published for the first time after Bolingbroke's death. There are four Essays so addressed : *Concerning the Nature, Extent, and Reality of Human Knowledge ; On the Folly and Presumption of Philosophers ; On the Rise and Progress of Monotheism ;* and *On Authority in matters of Religion.* Besides these, there is a letter occasioned by reading one of Archbishop Tillotson's Sermons, and a series of Fragments or Minutes of Essays, dealing with similar subjects, in a somewhat less connected form. As these works were published posthumously, their actual date has to be determined inferentially. In the Introduction to the first Essay the following statement occurs : " You have begun your Ethic Epistles in a masterly manner " (vol. v. p. 72, ed. 1809). The first instalment of the *Moral Essays* came out in 1730—that to the Earl of Burlington. To this, allusion seems to be made in Bolingbroke's Introductory Essay. The letters to Pope cannot, therefore, have been written earlier than 1731. They were most probably composed before their author retired to France in 1735, since he describes himself (p. 77, *op. cit.*) as " once more engaged in the

---

[1] Sichel, *Bolingbroke and His Time.* Vol. III., p. 450.

service of my country." They are very free in style. They
pretend to no seriousness or philosophic exactness. They
follow no very settled plan, but deal with a host of subjects
promiscuously, just as they arose in the mind. They show
all the author's wealth of illustration, the extent to which he
had dabbled in learning of various kinds, and they are by no
means deficient in rhetorical point and cleverness. But
there is nothing more to be said for them. They are wholly
uncritical, wholly one-sided, wholly unhistorical. They
abound in repetitions, contradictions, vehement and un-
bridled invective. They are actuated throughout by the
strongest possible bias, and, as we said above, they are
valueless from the point of view of the history of philosophy
or theology. It has been remarked by Lechler (*Gesch. d. Eng.
Deismus*, p. 369) that there is a certain similarity between
Bolingbroke and Chubb. Both are Deists, and both stand
outside the learned classes of their day. Both, therefore,
represent the influence of the speculations of the learned
upon the outer world : Chubb upon the industrial section,
Bolingbroke, upon the aristocratic section of it. Hence we
shall be disappointed if we expect anything in Bolingbroke's
writings but a tolerably able presentation of the current
Deistic thought.

It is not easy to give a connected account of the opinions
embodied in these incoherent and ill-arranged Essays.
Perhaps the clearest and best plan will be to illustrate from
them the principles which were most widely operative in the
Deistic writers at the time. It will be remembered that
Deism was one result of the effort to substitute Reason for
Authority as the ultimate source of truth. The Church had
claimed to define not only matters of faith, but also, to a
certain extent, questions of philosophy also. But the Reformation had shattered its authority in England. There
remained, therefore, two possibilities open : pure Individual-
ism, according to which each would determine his faith and

his philosophy for himself, without reference to any one; and Rationalism, which, while retaining the right of private judgment, fell back upon the faculty of reason for justification, presumably the same in all men. There was, therefore, a strong bias against all those positive additions to religion or to law which were not universal, but prevailed at particular times and places. Dogmas which went beyond what was called the Religion of Nature, and enactments which were superadded to the Law of Nature, came alike into disfavour. On all sides there was a clamour to return to primitive simplicity, to throw off the outgrowths upon the old faith and policy, and live again upon primeval lines. The appearance of dogmatic and metaphysical theology, and the promulgation of positive law were largely attributed to priestcraft and the cunning of the civil ruler. In defiance of the actual facts, it was maintained by many, by Bolingbroke among the number, that all the dogmatic theologians, from St. Paul downwards, were either madmen or knaves. The claims of theology were thus easily settled. But there was this modification in the case of law. Some positive enactments were absolutely necessary, though many might be assigned to the same motives as dogmatic Christianity. The State, therefore, and the State alone, was to fix these, their number and their import. To this function of defining the limits of positive law was naturally added that of fixing any positive form of religion, if it should be thought desirable. It might appear that it was to the advantage of a given State to make some uniform profession of religion: and so religion, like law, obtained from the State a precarious privilege to define itself, to a greater extent than would have been possible, if the point of view of Reason had been strictly maintained. These general principles seem to determine the thought of the time in its various stages. Let us see how they appear in Bolingbroke.

First, then, reason—the reason of the individual—is the

final judge in all causes, as well ecclesiastical as civil. It is "a gift of God, which is common to the whole species" (vol. v. p. 72). "He who examines on such principles as these, which are conformable to truth and reason, may lay aside at once the immense volumes of fathers and councils; of schoolmen, casuists, and controversial writers, which have perplexed the world so long" (*ibid.*, p. 106). "I rely on the authority of my cook when I eat my soup; on the authority of my apothecary when I take a dose of rhubarb; on that of Graham when I buy my watch; on that of Sir Isaac Newton when I believe in the doctrine of gravitation, because I am neither cook, apothecary, watchmaker, nor mathematician. But I am a rational creature, and am therefore obliged to judge for myself in all those cases where reason alone is the judge; the judge of the thing itself; for, even in the others, reason is the judge of the authority" (vol. vi. p. 272). Many other passages might be quoted, but these will probably be enough to show the primary position adopted by Bolingbroke.

If we ask for a further definition of the characteristics of rational knowledge, we find ourselves involved in some confusion. All human knowledge is *à posteriori*. "Human knowledge is not only posterior to the human system, but the very first elements of it are ideas which we perceive impressed by outward objects on our minds" (vol. v. p. 124). "It is such knowledge as we are fitted, by the organization of our bodies and the constitution of our minds to acquire. . . . It is knowledge for us. It is, in one word, human, and, relatively to us, when it is rightly pursued, real knowledge" (*ibid.*, pp. 126-7). "The first ideas with which the mind is furnished are received from without, and are caused by such sensations as the pressure of external objects excites in us, according to laws of passion and action which the Creator has established" (*ibid.*, p. 123). What these laws are, and how they work, we do not and cannot know. Per-

ception is passive, and is common to us with the animal
kind. When excited by the operation of external objects,
" the activity of the soul commences, and another source of
original ideas is opened ; for then we acquire ideas from,
and by the operation of, our minds" (*ibid.*, p. 135). At the
same time knowledge is closely limited. "Since simple
ideas are the foundation of human knowledge, this knowledge can neither be extended wider, nor elevated higher,
than in a certain proportion to them " (*ibid.*, p. 137). This
knowledge "goes no further than particular experiment,
and, as we attempt to make it general, we make it precarious. The reason is plain. It is a knowledge of particular effects, that have no connection nor dependency one
on another, even when they, or, more properly, the powers
that produce them, are united in the same substance ; and
of these powers, considered as causes, and not in their
effects, we have no means of attaining any knowledge at
all " (*ibid.*, p. 171). "General ideas are framed by the
' innate powers' of the mind, but are not ' taken with exactness from the nature of things on many occasions.'" . . .
" Ideas or notions are ill abstracted first, and ill compared
afterwards " (*ibid.*, p. 127). The method of science is induc-
tive (*ibid.*, p. 168), and leads only to insecure results. Hypotheses may be used sparingly, but it is hopeless to make
them, in all cases of real ignorance. "Is it reasonable,
when we cannot draw, from observation and experiment,
such conclusions as may be safe foundations on which to
proceed by the synthetic method in the pursuit of truth, to
assume certain principles . . . which have been never
proved, nor perhaps suggested by the phenomena, in hopes
that they may be so afterwards" (*ibid.*, p. 171). To secure
the acquisition of this precarious knowledge, the mind is
furnished with the two faculties of memory and association.
As to memory, Bolingbroke offers no explanation. He
rejects that offered by Descartes, and maintains that " the

only reasonable method we can take is to be content to know intuitively, and by inward observation, not the cause, but the effects of memory, and the use of it in the intellectual system" (*ibid.*, p. 139). The faculty of composition and of comparison of our ideas comes next, and is the result of the operation of Nature upon us. "Nature has united in distinct substances, as we commonly speak, various combinations of those qualities, each of which causes in us the sensation it is appropriated to cause, and our organs are fitted to receive; so that several, being thus combined and making their impression together, may be said to cause a complex sensation" (*ibid.*, p. 142). "The complex idea we have of every substance is nothing more than a combination of several sensible ideas, which determine the apparent nature of it to us" (*ibid.*, p. 144). Of all the ideas which the mind is capable of forming, its whole system of knowledge is composed: "and in the process of it, from first to last, we are assisted, directly or indirectly, by the lessons of nature" (*ibid.*, p. 145).

The influence of the rationalistic point of view upon psychology is very strongly marked here. Reason is paramount, but at the same time would seem to be the roughest and most uninstructed form of commonsense. The utterances of the sensational faculties are just taken as they are; no criticism is applied to them, and they are run together under various heads, without any attempt at explanation. This is Bolingbroke's own view of rational procedure. In virtue of it he dissents from Locke, whom he, for the most part, follows implicitly. The difference arises over the use of the word abstraction. "There is," says Bolingbroke, "a very practicable operation of the mind, by which we are said to abstract ideas, and by which we do in effect generalize them in a certain manner, and to a certain degree, by substituting one as representation of many. There is another— by which some philosophers have made themselves and others believe that they abstract, from a multitude of particular ideas, the idea of one general nature or essence, which is all of them, and none of them " (vol. vii. p. 298). This general idea of a thing Locke had called its nominal essence. " To talk of nominal essences and the abstraction of such comes too near the gibberish of the schools about genera and species ; the former method of abstracting or generalizing our ideas is the universal practice of mankind, the latter is purely imaginary " (vol. vii. p. 299). Such violent limitation of the operation of reason to the mental furniture with which every man, however ignorant or uneducated, is necessarily supplied, makes him entirely independent of, and incapable of entering into, any of the questions which have exercised philosophers in the past. They are survivals from the school of Plato, " who poisoned the very source of all real knowledge," of the " pompous jargon " of Aristotle, and others like him. They are maintained by men like Leibnitz, " one of the vainest and most chimerical men that ever got a name in philosophy." It would be interesting to collect the various abusive expressions bestowed by our author on philosophers ; but it would be quite impossible in a short notice, they would cover far too many pages.

As Bolingbroke has treated psychology " rationally," so he proceeds to treat ethics and theology. " The great principles of moral truth are as much founded in the nature of things as those of mathematical truth " (vol. vii. p. 340). Man is so constituted as to possess selfish and benevolent impulses from the first. The study of morality next to that of natural philosophy is, of all pursuits, that one which most deserves the application of the human mind. For " the will of God, in the constitution of our moral system, is the object of one; His infinite wisdom and power, that are manifested in the natural system of the universe, are the object of the other " (vol. v. p. 187). At the same time, here is no such thing as moral science properly so called. " Moral ideas and notions, of which no 'sensuous' copies can be made, which are held together in the mind, with the names assigned to them, by nothing but the retentive powers of the mind, and which can be signified by nothing but sounds that bear no resemblance to them, must fluctuate and vary, beget all the confusion, spread all the obscurity, and give occasion to all the fraud that I have mentioned " (vol. v. p. 217). As before, we were told that all our knowledge is closely limited to particulars, so here we are forbidden to attempt anything like a connected system of ethical principles. We shall know *à posteriori*, by experience of moral facts, what are the moral principles of our own age and country. Throughout the index of right and wrong, actions will be the advantage and disadvantage accruing from them (cf. Fragments and Minutes, No. II.).

On the subjects of religion and politics we may be very brief. Religion seems to have arisen (according to Bolingbroke) out of the curiosity of men to know the causes of phenomena which met their senses. They explain them as the actions of various beings very like themselves in nature, only much more powerful. Being wholly without the idea of secondary causes, they invent as many gods as they require. The first great principle of natural religion, though probably not the primitive faith of mankind (vol. vi. 38), " could not fail to be discovered as soon as some men began to contemplate themselves and all the objects that surrounded them " (vol. vi. p. 37). Not only is it so discoverable, it is actually demonstrable. The " demonstration " is given (vol. v. p. 123): " Since there must have been something from eternity, because there is something now, the eternal Being must be an intelligent Being, because there is intelligence now ; and such a Being must exist necessarily, whether things have been always as they are or whether they have been made in time, because it is

no more possible to conceive an infinite than a finite pro-
gression of effects without a cause. Thus the existence of
God is demonstrated, and cavil against demonstration is
impertinent." For the strenuous assertor of the *à posteriori*
character of human knowledge this seems a very remarkable piece of argument. Of God, as thus demonstrated into
existence, we know nothing whatever, save that He exists
and has created the world (vol. v. p. 60). Still it is " both
profane and injurious to true theism to assume the immediate presence and action of the supreme Being in all the
operations of corporal nature " (vol. vi. p. 91). He created
the world, but in what sense or how, nobody knows. The
knowledge of God is immediate and original in each of us,
reason being the instrument by which we obtain it ; and he
who " boasts a revelation superadded to reason to supply
the defects of it, is no less than mad " (vol. vi. pp. 170-1).
Miracles are obviously impossible. If they had ever
occurred, they must have carried the world into belief in
Christ and His revelation; " and yet, in fact, a universal
submission of all those, who were witnesses of the signs
and wonders that accompanied the publication of the
Gospel, did not follow " (vol. vi. p. 284). The miracles
are, therefore, false.

The causes of the growth of sects between the apostolical
age and this, are " to be found in the metaphysical madness
of philosophers mixing with the enthusiasm of the first
Christians, in the cabalistical practice of giving different
senses to the same passages of Holy Writ, in the uncertainty
of tradition, and in the use that a distinct order of men has
made, in every Christian state, of these and other circumstances to acquire a dominion over private consciences "
(vol. vi. p. 432). Christ republished natural religion together with the sanction of eternal punishment, and theologians since the days of Paul have been occupied in
falsifying Christ's message. It is worth noticing that in

his opinions about Saint Paul (vol. vi. p. 259, etc.) Bolingbroke anticipated in a way the views of Baur and his
school. He represents Saint Paul as preaching a completely new gospel, different from that of our Lord who
was sent to the Jews only (vol. vi. p. 369, etc.) and of the
earlier apostles, but he differs from the Tübingen school in
that he describes it as a fatal deflection from the truth.

It now remains only to indicate Bolingbroke's political
theory. "All societies," he writes, "were begun by instinct
and improved by experience" (vol. vii. p. 408). They take
their origin in those natural social conditions which are first
seen in the family. "We are led to civil through natural
society, and are fitted to be members of the one by having
been members of the other. This is the case of every one
in particular, and has been that of mankind collectively
considered" (vol. vii. p. 413).

The family, therefore, was the origin of the state. This
point of view, of course, makes Bolingbroke look with disfavour upon the speculations of Hobbes and Locke as to
the state of nature. Such theories, he says, represent
"mankind to themselves like a number of savage individuals out of all society in their natural state" (vol. vii.
p. 433), and this is not historical or philosophically
sound. So far the state is based on the law of nature.
"Nature begets natural law, natural law sociability,
sociability union of societies by consent, and this union by
consent the obligation of civil laws" (vol. vii. p. 376).
Under this civil obligation, definite forms of religion are
included: Erasmus, Plato, Varro, and some others, distinguished very rightly, "between the regard due to
religions already established, and the conduct to be held in
the establishment of them." They "thought that things
evidently false might deserve an outward respect, when
they are interwoven into a system of government." This
outward respect every good citizen will show them in such

a case, and they can claim no more in any. He will not propagate these errors, but he will be cautious how he propagates even truth in opposition to them (vol. v. p. 97).

Such, very briefly, is the philosophy of Lord Bolingbroke. In the short space allotted to this aspect of his life, it is entirely impossible to deal fully with his opinions. It might be interesting, if indeed it were worth while, to criticize elaborately the historical accounts of the progress of Christianity, etc., which are here passed by almost without mention, or it might be interesting to lay bare by means of analysis the sources from which he drew, and to trace the history of his philosophical terminology. But, after all, this would be treating him *au grand sérieux*—treatment which he scarcely deserves; philosophy and theology owe him nothing. He simply presents rationalism in its crudest form as it had filtered into his mind from without. We cannot wonder that publication of his works caused no stir in the learned world. We should have every reason to wonder if it had.

CHAPTER XI

CONCLUSION.

Bolingbroke seldom judged fairly—Why this is so—Hatred of Whigs—
Attacks on his private life—Severe criticism of his public career—The
Treaty of Utrecht a great work, and carried out by the Whigs—
Walpole's appreciation of Bolingbroke's foreign policy—The questions
of England's non-intervention on the Continent, of the importance of
the navy, of the value of the Colonies, treated of by Bolingbroke—
Carries out Cromwell's policy—Unfair attitude of Johnson and Burke
—The real value of Bolingbroke's writings—Popular view of his
character—Its absurdity—Summary of his work—The interest still
taken in his life—His claim to the title of "Great."

It is impossible to hope that the time has yet come when
either Bolingbroke's statesmanship or his own character
can be judged impartially. In the first place, the reigns of
Queen Anne and of the first two Georges are too near our
own times to allow us to regard without some party bias
the motives of men who guided or influenced England's
destinies less than two hundred years ago. When men
wax warm over the lives and characters of Charles I. and
Cromwell, it is too much to expect calm criticism of so
prominent a statesman as Bolingbroke. Then, again,
owing to the peculiar circumstances in which he was
placed, to the very unusual character of the political
problems with which he had to deal, he incurred the resentment of a large number of his Tory followers. A party
suffering under a serious defeat not unfrequently finds fault
with its leaders, and during the reign of George I. and the
greater part of that of George II. a large section of the
Tories blamed Bolingbroke for their comparative powerlessness, and altogether failed to appreciate at their proper

value the efforts he had made to place them in a position safe from the vicissitudes of party struggles.

Much adverse criticism has, too, been levelled at his memory in consequence of his adoption of the Deist position and of the publication of his rationalistic views. Probably his enemies, the Whigs, are mainly answerable for the bitter tone which has generally characterized the writings of historians and biographers of Bolingbroke. In the heat of conflict, the Jacobitism of a comparatively few Tories was magnified into a dangerous plot with wide ramifications. Fortune favoured the Whigs after the accession of George, and party exigencies demanded that they should continue to fasten on their opponents the stigma of Jacobitism. We know the result. The Tories remained hewers of wood and drawers of water for nearly half a century, and it is to this day well-nigh impossible to remove the general impression that Bolingbroke was throughout his career a firm adherent to the Jacobite cause. Bolingbroke himself declares that he expected as a matter of course to be impeached and attainted by the Whigs: what he did not expect was to be treated with ingratitude by the Tories; that ingratitude he characterized as " the last burst of the cloud," which has " gone near to overwhelm me."

" From our enemies," he says, " we expect evil treatment of every sort. We are prepared for it ; we are animated by it, and we sometimes triumph in it ; but when our friends abandon us, when they wound us, and when they take to do this an occasion when we stand the most in need of their support, and have the best title to it, the firmest mind finds it hard to resist."

But, though he regretted in his own day the attitude taken up towards him by a large section of that party in whose service he had, as he assures us, endeavoured to distinguish himself " under the immediate weight of great discouragement, and with the no very distant prospect of great danger," he was never careful to secure the favourable opinion of posterity. To stand well in the eyes of future generations was no object of his. "As to the opinion of mankind in general, and the judgment which posterity will pass on these matters, I am under no great concern—*suum cuique decus posteritas rependit.*"

His reputation as a statesman has been severely handled. The Peace of Utrecht is often styled shameful and disastrous. As that Treaty was Bolingbroke's masterpiece, his enemies have certainly shown wisdom in their generation in attacking it. But the Peace of Utrecht was, in its main features, an admirable settlement of the many difficult and complicated questions which had arisen during the long war, and Stanhope, Walpole, and their fellow Ministers, speedily showed a keen appreciation of the work of their rival by completing the pacification of Europe on the lines laid down by Bolingbroke. Walpole's system of Government, in fact, his whole policy at home and abroad, was based on the dynastic alliance between the Houses of Hanover and Bourbon. The preservation of the Peace of Utrecht became the aim of English, French, and Dutch Ministers. The Quadruple Alliance, by which the House of Austria relinquished its pretensions to Spain, the fall of Alberoni, the Treaties of Nystadt, Seville, and the second Treaty of Vienna (1731), were all brought about with the object of continuing that system which had been formed by the exertions of the great Tory statesman. Walpole also clearly recognized the economical and commercial value to England of Bolingbroke's foreign policy. The Whig Minister's long tenure of power was in great measure caused by the determined manner in which he clung to the Tory Peace policy. By doing so he enabled England to make rapid industrial progress, to extend her commerce, and to enjoy some twenty years of peace and prosperity. It was only when he followed this policy too slavishly, when he failed to grasp the fact that new problems had arisen which required fresh remedies, that public opinion demanded his overthrow.

The questions of England's interference or non-interference in Continental affairs, and of the relative importance of the army and navy to an insular power like Great Britain, are still much debated. Chatham and his great son, Canning, Lord Palmerston, and Lord Beaconsfield, all had definite views on these subjects. It would seem that the principles on which Bolingbroke acted are now beginning to receive universal acceptance. No part, however, of his foreign policy is more likely to be read with satisfaction than that which refers to the expansion of England. He secured for England a firm footing in North America, from which vantage-ground she was destined to put into execution, in less than ten years after his death, by the hand of one of his young patriot friends, a scheme which he had himself devised, and almost succeeded in carrying out. He was the first statesman who saw clearly the importance of checking the extension of the French power in Canada, and of giving a powerful impetus to the Colonial interests of Great Britain.

Though he failed to carry his commercial Treaty with France, he was successful in breaking through the Spanish monopoly of trade with South America. Cromwell had attempted in vain to penetrate the wall of religious fanaticism and commercial exclusiveness which closed the Spanish colonies to British trade; it was reserved for a man whose knowledge of foreign policy was far greater, and whose determination was fully as strong as that of the Protector, to effect an arrangement which for the first time allowed British trade, under certain conditions, with the Spanish colonies of South America. The verdict of history has now fully endorsed the wisdom and value of the Peace of Utrecht—a value which, as we have shown, was amply recognized by his great Whig rival.

His writings have been violently, and in many ways unfairly, attacked. Dr. Johnson and Burke are in great measure answerable for the popular opinions still in vogue with regard to his works. Dr. Johnson accused him of cowardice with reference to the publications of his philosophical speculations.

"Sir, he was a scoundrel and a coward : a scoundrel, for charging a blunderbuss against religion and morality ; a coward, because he had not resolution to fire it off himself, but left half-a-crown to a beggarly Scotchman (Mallet) to draw the trigger after his death."

The charge of cowardice contained in this famous sentence is amply refuted by the fact that Bolingbroke, during his lifetime, had never scrupled to publish criticisms, remarkable for their freedom, on religious subjects. Johnson, who was always looking for an opportunity for reviling Scotland and its inhabitants, may have been betrayed into this explosion more by the position of Mallet as literary executor than by his indignation at Bolingbroke's speculations. Burke is said to have inquired : "Who now reads Bolingbroke ?" The answer is obvious. Every lover of English composition in its most perfect form will read Bolingbroke. Every student of rhetoric will find his *Dissertation on Parties*, his *Spirit of Patriotism*, his *Idea of a Patriot King*, invaluable. To the historical student, a perusal of Bolingbroke's political writings is absolutely indispensable for a right comprehension of the ideas held by men of his day. Unless we know what men were thinking about in the times under consideration, the mere facts of history become dry bones. With the aid of Bolingbroke's political writings, the lives and thoughts of the men of his day are made real to us. Johnson and Burke in different fashion both owed much to Bolingbroke, and they repaid the debt by attempting to kick away the ladder which had aided their ascent to fame. Burke, indeed, owed more to Bolingbroke than he was perhaps aware of. "We do not," writes

Mr. Sichel, " accuse him (Burke) of deliberate plagiarism, but we convict him of unconscious assimilation. None would have been more surprised than Burke himself to find how saturated he was with the ideas, opinions, and language of one whom he was taught to slur and condemn."[1]

The attacks on his private life, on his public career, and on the value of his literary works contain much that is unanswerable. But most of Bolingbroke's biographers have either approached the subject of their biography with undisguised hostility, or, by enlarging on unimportant details in his career, have failed to place in their proper proportion his greatest political and literary achievements. One biographer, whose whole tone has been, till quite lately, that generally adopted by historians, speaks of the " ingrate and cankered Bolingbroke," of his " fell genius," his " subtle intellect, his showy, sophistical eloquence, his power of intrigue, his consummate falsehood, his vice and infidelity," and concludes, somewhat charitably, by styling him a " superior fiend " and by quoting Milton's lines :—

> " In act more graceful than humane,
> A fairer person lost not heaven ; he seemed
> For dignity composed and high exploit ;
> But all was false and hollow, though his tongue
> Dropt manna, and could make the worst appear
> The better reason, to perplex and dash
> Maturest counsels."

Now, a " superior fiend " would not have stood in an agony of grief at Pope's bedside. " Fell geniuses " do not watch puppet-shows with little girls on their knees. " Ingrate and cankered " politicians do not write anxious letters about sick nephews and offer to pay their debts. But it is not worth while to say more on this subject. These views, quoted above, merely show the extent to which calumny, vindictiveness, and malice will pursue the memory of an

---

[1] Sichel, *Bolingbroke and His Times.* Vol. II., p. 447.

illustrious statesman. His faults are patent enough, but so are his virtues. He must have been a delightful companion.

Swift, in a passage already quoted, bears full witness to his good-nature, his generosity, his excellent taste, his wit, capacity, good looks, quickness of apprehension, and learning. But he had the misfortune to offend mortally the great Whig families, and the hostility of that Venetian oligarchy, which seldom forgave, pursued him through his life and after his death with relentless fury. The great Whig families had, indeed, no cause to love the memory of Bolingbroke. In 1714 he had seriously threatened the success of their Revolution principles, and he had almost ruined their schemes; during Walpole's Ministry he had undermined their monopoly of power, and he had shown the Tories the way to oust them from office and to consign them to the cold shade of opposition during most of George III.'s and all George IV.'s reign. Could he expect any mercy from Whig historians?

No greater compliment could perhaps be paid to his memory than the interest which is still taken in his meteoric career, in his soaring ambition, in his keen literary tastes. As long as there remains a classical scholar, so long may we look for translations of Homer; as long as mediæval history is studied, fresh monographs on Dante and his divine poem will continue to appear. And we may say that as long as human nature with its lights and shades still occupies the attention of men in each succeeding generation, writers will be found ready to make fresh studies of this extraordinary character, in which, as Lord Chesterfield said, "good and evil were perpetually jostling one another." Most of his contemporaries are allowed to sleep in comparative peace; but who can say that the final word has been said of the author of the Peace of Utrecht? His illustrious ancestry, his fiery ambition, his remarkable and diversified talents, his position at the head of affairs at one of the most momentous crises in English history, his sudden and most dramatic fall, all lend a deep interest to Anne's reign. Then his desertion by the Fates, his banishment into perpetual opposition just when his powers were at their best, his struggles against the Whig families, his laborious attempts to reconstruct the Tory party, all give the domestic history of George II. a special interest.

His age was the age of great men. Marlborough, Somers, Shrewsbury, Godolphin, Harley, Walpole, Swift, Pope, Pulteney, and Carteret were all his contemporaries. It was an age of political and literary giants. Seldom has England been possessed at any one epoch of so much political talent. But Bolingbroke towers above them all in those qualities which make a statesman. In his power of grasping opportunities, in his splendid abilities, in his marvellous oratory, in his endeavour to elevate and expand the views of men, he was far superior to any of his contemporaries. Once only did he lose his head, and for that fatal error England paid dearly. The author of the Peace of Utrecht, and of the reconstruction of the Tory party, the advocate of Parliamentary freedom, and of the union of the people and the King, may well be pardoned one error in judgment. " Lord Bolingbroke," said Disraeli in 1832, was " one of the ablest men who ever lived." The recognition of his merits by French writers shows that Bolingbroke's diversified talents are appreciated beyond England's four seas. " His name," it has been said, " may be tracked in history by a luminous streak, such as a shooting star leaves behind it in its glancing and glittering dash across the sky." Whatever view is taken of certain episodes in his career, no one will now dispute his title of The Great Lord Bolingbroke.

INDEX.

A

BILLING AND SONS, LTD., PRINTERS, GUILDFORD, ENGLAND